I WAS A REALLY

GOOD MOM

before I HAD KIDS

I WAS A REALLY
GOOD MOM
before I HAD KIDS

• • •

Reinventing Modern Motherhood

Trisha Ashworth and **Amy Nobile**

CHRONICLE BOOKS
SAN FRANCISCO

Library of Congress Cataloging-in-Publication Data available.
ISBN-10: 0-8118-5650-X
ISBN-13: 978-0-8118-5650-8

Manufactured in Canada.

Design by bonnie berry design

Some names in this book have been changed at the subjects' request.

Distributed in Canada by Raincoast Books
9050 Shaughnessy Street
Vancouver, British Columbia V6P 6E5

10 9 8 7 6 5 4 3 2 1

Chronicle Books LLC
680 Second Street
San Francisco, California 94107
www.chroniclebooks.com

For Alex, Pierce, Julia, Sam, and Emily; we simply adore you.
And for Paul and Eric, for being what matters most.

CONTENTS

CHAPTER I

THE FAKE-CUPCAKE PROBLEM

○ ○ ○

(Why We Needed
to Write This Book)

quiz no. 1

DOES THIS SOUND LIKE YOU?

CHECK ALL THAT APPLY.

- [ ] You secretly wish you had your own apartment.

- [ ] If you have to play Go Fish one more time, you will definitely poke your eyeballs out.

- [ ] You lie to your friends about how much babysitting help you have.

- [ ] Next time your husband goes to Home Depot to "help" you, you think he should just stay there.

- [ ] You feel guilty that you like going to work so much.

- [ ] You worry about whether your son's lunch box is the "right" one.

- [ ] You dread the question "What do you do all day?"

- [ ] You consider a trip to the dentist your special "alone time."

- [ ] You plan to get control over your life . . . next week.

- [ ] Reading before bed feels like a luxury.

- [ ] You find that slowly browsing the aisles at Target, by yourself, is better than therapy.

IF YOU'RE SITTING DOWN AND READING THIS, THEN YOU MUST not be having the worst day ever. Or maybe you are. Whatever kind of day you're having—you couldn't love your kids more, or you couldn't be more eager to jump in your car and speed away—we've been there. Between us we have five kids, two husbands, two dogs, three-quarters of a career, steadily improving skills at negotiating with toddlers, and way too much stress. This book got started on one of those nights that followed one of those days—dog poop tracked into the house, wild children in the aisles of Target. Laser-eyed, we watched our clocks until 4 P.M. Then we each poured ourselves a glass of wine and picked up the phone to call each other.

As we talked, our kids tattooed one another with permanent markers and played in the dog-food bowls. Whatever—it really didn't matter. We discussed our days, and within ten minutes we'd laughed, cried, whined about our husbands, wondered what happened to our sex drives, snapped at the kids, wished we had passions, and questioned why we sometimes felt like bad moms. Were you a bad mom if you screamed at a four-year-old for getting up twelve times in one night? Were you a good mom if you stayed up late baking fifty cupcakes for the next day's ballet recital? Would passing off store-bought cupcakes as homemade really be a terrible offense?

Meanwhile we were trying to turn the three ingredients in our respective refrigerators into some semblance of dinner. And our husbands, who'd finally come home, were looking at us cross-eyed for yet again being on the phone. Granted, blabbing while the kids trashed the house might not have looked so good from their position. But immediately hanging up to resume our roles as moms would not have been a good idea, either. These phone chats were our salvation.

"OH, REALLY? YOU'RE HAVING A HARD TIME?" . . . *CLICK.*

Why did we need these daily chats? Because we needed to vent. Badly. Our husbands didn't understand the fake-cupcake problem. Nor did our mothers. Nor did our kids.

Our chats started five days after one of us (OK, Amy) had her first baby. It wasn't pretty—massive exhaustion, recurrent mastitis—and what did one of her closest friends do? She pulled that dirty motherhood-perfectionist trick.

"Oh, really? You're having a hard time? I always felt great. That never happened to me."

Click.

So we began talking to each other. Our lives weren't identical. Years earlier, before motherhood, we'd both established careers, but one of us was now a stay-at-home mom, and the other a part-time working mom. Still, we felt exactly the same way: questioning our choices, grappling with guilt, and wondering if the other mothers we knew were struggling to keep it together, too.

Once we started being honest about how we felt, it was addictive.

DIRTY LITTLE SECRET

My girlfriends and I decided that 4 P.M. is the "new 5" when it comes to pouring that first glass of wine every day.

The truth is, we did so much talking to each other and felt so much better afterward that we started to think we should write down some of what we were saying. One of us had a public relations background and the other had had a career in advertising, so we wiped off our whiteboards and brainstormed about all the issues that moms today face. Our goal: to try to understand phenomena like the fake-cupcake problem by reverse-engineering them back to their component parts: 2 cups guilt, ½ cup competition, 2 tablespoons judgment, ½ teaspoon trying to live in the moment, et cetera.

Here's what we came up with:

- As mothers, we put way too much pressure on ourselves.
- We have an unrealistic image of what a "good" mom is.
- We secretly compare ourselves to other moms, who seem to have it all together.
- We think we need to be perfect all the time.
- We feel alone.
- Our lives feel out of balance.

We also had some fairly major questions:

- What happened to the people we were before we became moms?
- Why did our marriages change when we became parents?
- Why, no matter what choice we make, do we constantly feel that we've made the wrong one?
- Why do we feel guilty all the time?
- How come nobody talks about how hard motherhood truly is?

Then we started to wonder if we, in particular, were just more insecure and screwed up than most mothers.

So we decided to look for some answers. We started asking everybody we knew.

EXCUSE ME, YOU'RE JACK'S MOM, RIGHT?
ARE YOU LOSING YOUR MIND?

It can be slightly embarrassing to be women on a mission, particularly if that mission involves asking taboo questions of vague acquaintances. Still, we decided to start asking every mom we could find how she was feeling. In the grocery store, at after-school pick-up, during cocktail parties, and while pushing swings at the playground. Even in the middle of yoga class:

(During Downward Dog)

Trisha: *Psssst, Liz. How's it going? Are you losing it?*

Liz: Yeah, I'm gonna shoot myself in the head.

Talk to ya after class!

We realized that we were on to something.

Over the course of the next six months, we talked to more than a hundred women, logging six thousand minutes of intense, sometimes tearful, sometimes humorous interviews. We talked to women across the country, from small towns like Port Angeles, Washington, to big cities like Boston. We talked to stay-at-home moms, full-time working moms, and part-time working moms. We talked to mothers in their late twenties and in their early forties. We talked to married mothers and single mothers. We talked to mothers with one child, mothers with two children, and mothers with three, four, and five. Ninety-five percent of our research was done one-on-one, in person and on the phone. We sat down with women behind closed doors or found some quiet time on the phone, and we listened. Many mothers threw us a bucket of sunshine at first, but then gave themselves permission to reveal their honest feelings about how they're living in motherhood today. Many told their truths for the first time in years, and in doing so, they felt instant relief.

OK, not quite *instant*. Getting to the relief took a few minutes. Twenty-two minutes, to be exact.

Us: *Tell us a little something about yourself.*

Them: Well, I'm thirty-six, I have two kids, and I used to be the manager of a pharmaceutical company. I finally got a big promotion right before I had my first child.

After having kids, I missed having control over my day. I know it might sound selfish, but that's how I felt. Every day I felt defeated . . . keeping the house clean, feeding the kids, getting birthday-party gifts, serving dinner, bathing the kids. . . . And my husband expects me to be happy. So I just be with my kids, don't complain, and try and feel lucky.

Lori / 2 children, Los Angeles, CA

Us: *How are you handling motherhood right now?*

Them: It's amazing. I love it! I am *so* balanced. My husband is my *best* friend. I feel *really* blessed and *extremely* lucky that I have healthy kids and we're able to provide a great foundation and a positive environment for our children.

Twenty-two minutes later:

Us: *Sounds like you have real balance in your life. A lot of women we've talked to seem to have a hard time finding that. How do you do it?*

Them: Ummm, well, maybe *balance* isn't the right word. *[Long pause.]* Umm, actually, I haven't taken a shower in three days. And, OK, my husband and I haven't had sex in three weeks. And, well, the laundry is piled to the ceiling, and my house is a mess. My five-year-old daughter could also use a serious attitude adjustment. I really wish I had time to get a haircut. And I hate to admit it, but my son's first word was "Shrek."

Us: OK, *things aren't perfect. But overall, are you happy?*

Them: Umm, wow, *happy?* Well, yeah. I mean, yeah, I'm happy. Well, I wouldn't say *totally* happy. You know, I have an MBA. Why can't I do this? *[Long pause.]* I feel like such a bad mom sometimes. This really isn't what I expected.

One mother—talking with us on the phone, between working and picking up her four-year-old from preschool—summed it up best: "I was a really good mom before I had kids."

I thought I'd fall in love with my baby and it would complete my life. It wasn't that way for me. There's a lot of pressure on women to feel that this is the end-all-and-be-all when you have that baby.

Christy / 1 child, Richmond, VA

SHOULD I GET HER A SOCCER TUTOR?

After talking to mothers nationwide, we realized that we, collectively, needed to get a grip on ourselves. If we were to love motherhood as much as we love our children, the first step was to start being completely honest—honest about ourselves, honest with our families, honest with one another.

Honesty is tough. We know—we still put on the occasional "happy face" for even our closest friends. We'd also rather accentuate the positive than the negative. But you can't fix a problem you don't admit exists. So here we go. This is our truth:

We love being mothers, we love our children (especially when they're sleeping), but . . .

o We are *overwhelmed.*

o We feel *guilty* for everything that we don't do or could have done better.

o We feel *stretched* beyond belief.

A lot of times, if I need to cry, I'll just do it alone. We feel like we don't have permission to say, "Wait a minute, this isn't all it was supposed to be." Or "Is this all there is?" Or "I don't have the right training for this job!"

PATRICIA / 2 CHILDREN, SAN DIEGO, CA

- We *judge* ourselves for being unable to accomplish everything we set out to do.
- We *compare* ourselves to others who we think have it all together.
- We feel *out of control.*
- We have more "bad mom" days than we care to admit.
- We are struggling to find *balance* (if it even exists).
- We've lost sight of our *identity.*
- We feel *alone* because no one talks honestly about how they really feel.

At first, we were just perplexed at how hard motherhood was for all of us. *Why?* Women have been doing this forever. Literally. And we have the advantages of disposable diapers, TiVo, sippy cups, birth control, and equal rights.

Then we had our first epiphany: *The problem is all the choices.*

Yes, we are very grateful for the women who fought and worked so hard to give us all these advantages. The feminist movement opened doors, enabling and inspiring us to go for what we truly want in life. But the women's movement, as far as we're concerned, is still a work in progress. Self-actualization is a lot easier to talk about than it is to attain. How to "do it"—to be empowered, to take our own lives by the reins, to have children and be happy, all at the same time—is something most of us have yet to figure out.

A very large part of the how-to-do-it problem is all the pressure we put on ourselves. We were told by our parents we could, and should, "do it all," and we took them seriously.

Which led us to our next epiphany. Nearly all the women we spoke to had the same core problem: *insane expectations.*

What do we mean by *insane?* Our generation's definition of what a good mom is—or what it takes to be a good mom—is nearly impossible to fulfill. When expectations (society's, our husbands', our friends', and our own) are insane, we constantly feel like we're not succeeding.

One mom, Monica, says it well: "I feel overwhelmed. I never feel quite together enough. I feel like, 'Why can't I do it?' I look around and think everyone's perfect—and then there's me. I feel like I can't just have kids. I have to have brilliant, talented, perfect kids, and only then have I begun to be a good mother. If my kid is not in the top math class or the best at soccer, I have failed. I think, should I get her a soccer tutor?"

I thought having a baby would be like having a pet—oh, this will be cute, we'll be this happy little family.

Kim / 3 children, Madison, NJ

When we talked to women about their lives, they talked to us about feeling trapped. One mother we interviewed put it like this: "I am constantly questioning my decisions. It's hard. I have a great education; I had a great job. If I stay home with my child, I feel like, 'Is this all there is?' and if I work, I feel consumed with guilt. So I end up feeling trapped, like I can't win."

I WAS SO THROWN OFF BY THIS SEVEN-POUND PERSON

Part of the reason it's so hard to start talking honestly about motherhood is that we feel like we're failing, and that's deeply embarrassing. We've had all the choice in the world, so if we're not pleased with the path we're on, it's our own damn fault, right?

A lot of women told us they thought they were supposed to have an innate talent for motherhood, and they felt surprised and frustrated that mothering is so difficult. As one mom put it, "There's a myth that we're so highly developed and we can handle anything, but having a baby is destabilizing. I was so thrown off by this seven-pound person who I couldn't figure out! There are plenty of times I don't want to be around my kids. Maybe I'm not patient enough. What does this say about me if [motherhood] doesn't entirely fulfill me?"

The sheer magnitude of the mothering job also trips us up. Nobody, of course, tells you this before the baby arrives, but as a mom you're supposed to be an accountant, chauffeur, personal trainer, hygienist, interior decorator, camp counselor, servant, chef, personnel manager, and cheerleader. And you have job "reviews"—emotional, impolite ones, several times a day, offered up by little bosses who believe that you're "mean" if you stop the cookie binge at seven. Your working conditions are substandard. You can't call in sick. What's more, even if you're riddled with questions and self-doubt, nobody wants to hear it if you're on the brink. Queries like "How was your day?" or "How are you doing?" are not meant to be answered honestly. They're meant to be answered with words like *good, great,* or *fine.* Because, really, what are Dad and the kids going to do if Mommy says, "My day was terrible"? Or what would happen if Mommy replied, "Yeah, well, I'm burnt out, and I quit"?

HONESTY STARTS HERE

Sure, you can go ahead and keep telling all the women in your book group how beautiful your whole life is, but for us, it's time for a reality check. We didn't realize that being mothers would make us feel so unsuccessful. We didn't realize that motherhood would involve so many sacrifices. We didn't know we'd lose control. We didn't know the skills we honed at work would not be transferable or, worse, would be transferable in really unappealing ways. As one mom told us, "I used to be a creative art director at a big ad agency, and I found myself driving around to six different drugstores at 10 P.M. to find three specific flavors of Kool-Aid to match the color theme of my daughter's birthday party."

We've been there, done that. And we can tell you from experience: this is not who this woman thought she'd turn out to be.

So it's time to get real and start improving our lives in motherhood. And the first step involves being frank—with ourselves and with others. More than one hundred moms shared their innermost thoughts with us. They admitted some dirty little secrets and offered advice, which you'll find throughout the book. We've pinpointed eight core issues to talk about, and each one stems from the same source: our overblown expectations. At the end of each chapter you will find applicable solutions that will help you rewrite your own rules for living in modern motherhood.

First, we need to get some disclaimers out of the way.

- Yes, we all love our kids.
- Yes, we all adore our husbands.
- Yes, we are very, very lucky to have so many choices.

Yet . . .

- We're feeling pretty maxed out right now.
- We're stuck. We need to think about motherhood in a new way.
- We sometimes resent being mothers.
- We want to feel better about our lives.

The hope is that we'll raise great kids *and* be happy doing it. And that means talking about the good and bad sides of motherhood. Because if we can talk honestly, perhaps we can lose the notion that we can and should do it all. And if we can lose that notion, then perhaps we can get a grip on our insane expectations. And if we can get a grip on our insane expectations, perhaps we can stop judging ourselves and other moms, learn to say no when we need to, embrace our daily lives, nurture ourselves and our husbands, and maybe, just maybe, relax and find peace. The ideal is to be true to ourselves, to make conscious choices based on our own value systems (and not others' expectations of us), and to live our lives in ways that serve our own best interests and those of our families. Only then can we begin to love motherhood as much as we love our children.

CHAPTER 2

I LOVE BEING A MOM; I JUST HATE DOING IT

. . .

(Align Your Expectations With Reality)

quiz no. 2

FOR YOU TO FEEL LIKE A GOOD
MOM, WHICH OF THE FOLLOWING
DO YOU NEED TO DO?

CHECK ALL THAT APPLY.

- [ ] Patiently read four bedtime stories each night to each kid.

- [ ] Bake homemade cakes for each child's birthday.

- [ ] Organize and neatly store all toys at the end of the day.

- [ ] Raise your voice only if someone's on fire.

- [ ] Look and feel happy, and look as if looking and feeling that way takes no effort.

- [ ] Instill perfect manners in your children.

- [ ] Ignore your own needs when the children need you.

- [ ] Prepare healthful, homemade meals and see them consumed three times a day.

- [ ] Teach your children to swim, read, and tie their own shoes before kindergarten.

- [ ] Do it all. Do it all perfectly.

"HAPPINESS." SUCH A BIG WORD. KIND OF INTIMIDATING, IN FACT. Mostly because it's what we all really want. You can say you want a new car, or a manicure, or your husband to come home and whip up dinner. But deep down inside, what we really want is to be happy. Or, we should say, what we really want is to raise happy kids and be happy doing it. We also want to get enough sleep. But happiness is the main goal and probably the more attainable one, too.

We asked a lot of mothers if they were happy. And we heard a lot of stuttering.

> Us: *Are you happy?*
>
> Them: Am I happy? Yeah . . . *[Sounds hesitant.]* Am I like the happiest I've ever been? I don't know. I just feel stressed a lot, all the responsibility of motherhood. . . . Should I be the happiest? That's the hard thing. When you plan your wedding and have a baby, there's an expectation that this is the happiest time of your life. And it's not! There's resentment of giving up the life that you had. It's not about you anymore. I wish I had known that having a baby is not the happiest time of your life. It's hard. There's a lot of sacrifice.

Some mothers, when we asked if they were happy, didn't even seem to fully understand the question.

Us: *Are you happy?*

Them: "What do you mean, happy? Like *happy* happy, or just kind of happy?"

        "Am I happy? Umm, yeah, I'm pretty happy. Yeah."

        "Happy . . . What does that really mean?"

        "Happy? I never really thought about it. Am I happy? I'm not ecstatic. I'm stressed."

        "*Happy* is not a good word for me. The word that describes me best is *challenged*."

Whether or not my husband will admit it, I think he has certain expectations of me. Like the dinner thing. I absolutely hate it. Hate it, hate it, hate it. And he was always the cook, always the one who would whip up any meal. But when his work started revving up, things changed, and he would insinuate that we hadn't had a good meal in days. And I just lost it. I felt like I was letting the family down. So I added that to my list of things I needed to do.

Andrea / 2 children, St. Louis, MO

As we know from our own experience, and from listening to more than one hundred otherwise articulate women sputtering, it can be hard to just come out and say, *"I'm not that happy."* Partly because admitting this tends to really open the floodgates, and that can be scary. And partly because questioning our happiness feels like failure.

We heard it again and again, from dozens of moms coast to coast: there's a lot of pressure to be happy, to maintain appearances. No one

DIRTY LITTLE SECRET

I'm continually running away from my children. I love them, but they just drain me. There's a poof of smoke at 2:30 P.M. when my help arrives and I fly out the door.

feels permission to be unhappy. Everyone feels a lot of pressure to love being a mom. In fact, loving being a mom all the time seems to be an integral part of the "mom" job description: take care of your children, put your own needs aside, keep everybody happy, and be happy yourself.

I RESENT THAT QUESTION

It can drive you crazy, trying to look and, more importantly, act blissed out when you're not. And the pressure to seem pleased does not come just from our spouses and the other moms around town. It also comes from ourselves. *We* feel we should be happy in motherhood, and a lot of times we are, but we still get down on ourselves for the times we're not. Moreover, we feel we have no right to not like this job or to admit how hard it is. And one of the surest ways to go from being a little unhappy to being really unhappy is to start getting down on yourself for not being happy in the first place.

Ultimately, I am not the kind of mom I thought I'd be. I pictured myself baking cookies and singing songs with my sweet girls, and my house would be perfectly organized with color-coordinated bins. Instead, I'm kind of in this fuzzy haze of I don't know what. I can't remember what I did yesterday.

Paulina / 2 children, Boulder, CO

Actress Felicity Huffman, wife of actor William H. Macy and mother of his children, spoke for a lot of us when she recently turned a question back on *60 Minutes* interviewer Lesley Stahl:

Stahl: Is motherhood the best experience of your life?

Huffman: No. No, and I resent that question. Because I think it puts women in an untenable position. Because unless I say to you, "Oh, Lesley, it's the best thing I've ever done with my whole life," I'm considered a bad mother.

So let's be upfront about it: motherhood can be humbling, inspiring, rewarding, exhausting, boring, banal, dirty, and up-and-down. It's also way too out-of-control an experience to discuss in unnuanced, romanticized terms. Motherhood is a great joy and also a great burden. It does not leave us all consistently happy or completely fulfilled. Furthermore, we're tired of the notion that motherhood should make us happy, and we're tired of trying to live up to the ideal that "good moms are happy moms." Because if we've agreed that the only way to be a "good" mother is to be having the best experience of our lives, how can we possibly have an honest conversation about what it's like to raise kids?

One mother really summed it up when she said, "I love being a mom; I just hate doing it."

I feel like my life has eight slices of pie and my plate only holds six. It's constant triage.

Kristy / 4 children, Mill Valley, CA

Let's pause here. This is an amazingly honest thing to say—*I love being a mom; I just hate doing it*. And it's all the more amazing because it resonates with so many of us. Why? We love our children, and we love being their mothers, but sometimes we just hate doing "it" because "it," as we've defined it, is an impossible job. We're not talking about the indignities of wiping up runny noses or runny diarrhea—we expected as much. We're talking about the crushing exhaustion, gerbil-on-a-flywheel feeling of every day. We're talking about the failure we feel when we can't bring ourselves to make a Halloween costume, even though that very day we rushed out of work early to make it to a Mommy & Me music class. We're talking about the sinking feeling we have when we finally get into bed at night, knowing that we've failed to perform competently (according to ourselves) on yet another day. Those parentheses are very important: we're labeling our own selves failures.

Motherhood is one of those things that's totally impossible to picture until it happens to you. You think it will be a certain way—you won't yell at your kids, you'll have infinite patience, you'll sit on the floor for hours reading to your kids, you'll divide the parenting duties fairly with your husband—and then, boom, your baby arrives and your whole world turns upside down. I mean, I always pictured myself with kids, but I didn't expect to be barely keeping it together 99 percent of the time. The days just flow together, and I'm supposed to cherish it all?

VICTORIA / 2 CHILDREN, OAKLAND, CA

Which raises some interesting questions. Like, why did we give ourselves such impossible standards? And why are so many of us—smart, sensible women—having such a hard time managing one of the most primal occupations on earth?

EXPECTATIONS, THE MOTHER OF ALL PROBLEMS

After hundreds of hours on the phone with dozens of women around the country, we started to recognize a pattern. Nine times out of ten, if a woman was unhappy in motherhood, her expectations were overblown. Working mothers *expected* they'd be able to do it all, and they felt like failures when they couldn't. Stay-at-home moms *expected* that they'd stay sane kneeling on the floor twelve hours a day and that they'd feel *lucky* doing it.

We heard a lot of delusional thinking leading to a lot of delusional expectations:

- Motherhood will slide right into my life.
- With a few little tweaks, my career will stay on track.
- I'll be completely fulfilled by my children as a stay-at-home mom.
- If I try hard enough, I can balance it all.
- Once I become a mother, I will become a more nurturing, selfless, giving person.
- I will be able to handle motherhood pretty easily.

No matter a mother's age, where she lived, or how many kids she had, we heard the same themes. "I feel too guilty to hire a babysitter." "I'm so stressed, my head is going to pop off." We also heard a lot of stories like, say, the one about a mom in the kitchen at 7:15 A.M., having been awake for two hours, trying to bake cookies in time to pack them in preschool lunches, marinate fish for dinner, and vacuum crushed Cheerios off the floor. This mom is maxed, on autopilot, and almost certainly in a funk.

She's also too busy to do the one thing that would make her day a whole lot better—stop to ask herself, "Am I doing too much, and why?"

Asking this simple question is the first step in realigning expectations and thus becoming a happier mom. We're the first to admit, expectations aren't that easy to corral. But the good news here is that, unlike the whims of a three-year-old, expectations are technically possible to pin down and control. The goal is to align your expectations with your reality. If we expect to make dinner seven nights a week, if we expect to home-bake the cookies, if we expect to never lose our tempers, if we expect to never need time for ourselves, if we expect to be happy every single day, we will set ourselves up for failure.

I have tremendous pressure from all ends. A lot of it is self-imposed. I feel like I'm trying to be perfect in so many ways: spend as much quality time with my kids as I can, be a supportive wife, still keep my career on target. The standard is very high. The majority of women in my community look perfect all the time, seem so fit and healthy. They act like decorating the house for Thanksgiving is the best thing in their lives.

Monica / 2 children, Los Angeles, CA

Truly, we found that no matter where a woman fell on the motherhood "angst" scale, all roads led back to expectations. Happy mothers had realistic expectations. Unhappy mothers had untenable ones.

DIRTY LITTLE SECRET

I lost my job but still dropped my son off at day care and pretended to look for a job while I went shopping and got a manicure.

> I don't have time to hug my husband. It's not on my to-do list.
>
> Jenn / 2 children, San Anselmo, CA

WHO WOULD HAVE KIDS IF THEY REALLY KNEW?

Studies have shown that humans find it physiologically impossible to remember pain, so after we have had our first child (or second or third), we might encourage our friends to do the same. Although we also seem unable to remember and convey to our friends what the early weeks and months of parenting are actually like, many new moms felt betrayed by their friends' omissions. "I remember nothing about how difficult it was to be a new mother," Sarah, a mother of two young boys in San Francisco, told us. "It's like I just purged the memory banks because those times were so hard. Similarly, my mother comes over and can't understand why my children are so wild. 'You three were *never* like this. You were perfect angels.' It's not catty or ill-intentioned. It's just memory loss—or the biological imperative. Who would have kids if they really knew?"

> My husband's expectations are higher for me after I decided to stay home. I feel like he expects me to be happier. I get to raise our kids, so I should be happy, right? I can't really complain, so I turn into a martyr. I don't even realize I'm doing it, but he does. He says, "Get more help if you need it." But I know that if I did, it would feel like I wasn't doing my job.
>
> Laura / 2 children, Los Angeles, CA

DIRTY LITTLE SECRET

Sometimes I think, "I can't believe I gave up nine months of drinking for *this*."

Likewise, for many, the reality that staying home with children full-time is not totally satisfying came as a surprise. These stay-at-home moms didn't realize how much their identities were tied to their careers. They didn't realize how much their professional selves were their primary source of feeling successful and fulfilled. One mom in New York told a common story: privileged enough to stay home after having kids, aware that this is a gift, yet struggling nonetheless. "I had worked really hard for ten solid years, and staying home with my son was kind of cushy at first! But I got depressed soon after. For the first time since I left my parents' house at eighteen, I didn't have a job and I wasn't making money. It was weird asking my husband for money! I went into this self-loathing period. When you're a mother, nobody's saying, 'You're doing a great job; you're so great; what initiative, mopping up that vomit!'"

I have an older sister who was born for motherhood, so she didn't really warn me about it. I only heard the good. Then when I became a mom, I had to make so many sacrifices. My mom never complained and never told me about the harsh reality. I was totally unprepared.

Karen / 2 children, Pittsburgh, PA

Working moms are confronting a different reality. Many of these women feel they have no time for themselves—no time to eat, no time to work out, no time ever to just sit and breathe—and they are realizing that this is no way to live. Many working moms told us they're feeling stretched so thin they're going to crack. They told us they feel they have so many different roles to play that it's nearly impossible to dress their part. For instance, one working mom, a lawyer, told us about a day not so long ago when she had to go to court. She dressed up in pantyhose, makeup, a navy blue suit, and her "new going-back-to-work heels." At lunch, when she raced home to check on her family's new puppy, he leapt on her with muddy paws. Next she had to run to school to pick up a car-pool of eight kids. "So I get out of my car and I'm frantically putting up seats. And I rip the entire back seam of my skirt! I'm covered in mud, my butt is sticking out of my skirt, I'm sweating, and all of these moms are staring at me. Why am I even trying? *You can't do it all.*"

REALIGNING EXPECTATIONS WITH REALITY

Certainly, a mother cannot skip feeding her family or retreat into utter sloth. But as a first step toward happiness, she can start being really aware and really deliberate about the expectations she takes on. Granted, redefining motherhood is no small task, especially since our heads seem to be filled to the brim with other people's opinions of the kinds of mothers we should be. The idea here is to create our own (realistic) vision of motherhood and work toward that, instead of trying to achieve some grandiose nonsense that's probably not attainable and most likely not what we really want.

I had to prioritize and make choices based on what's important for our family. For instance, I made a commitment to go to every doctor's appointment with my daughter. I chose a pediatrician who is closer to my office than our house, so I *can* do that. I really have tried to be thoughtful about some of those decisions. I have friends who ask, "Are you going to put your daughter in preschool?" I say, "I don't know if that is going to work. It will add too much running around." In the past, I would have just gotten caught up in what everyone else was doing. Now we really try to stay within the boundaries of what works for our family.

Jane / 2 children, Atlanta, GA

The Never-Ending To-Do List

A good place to start realigning your expectations is your to-do list. Many women we talked to, like us, have impossibly long lists. Here's a partial list of things mothers told us they *had* to do:

1. Spend quality time, separately, with each of their kids

2. Spend quality time with their close friends and family

3. Look refreshed, relaxed, fit, and fashionable on a shoestring budget and no sleep

4. Cook a good, nutritious dinner every night, and get the kids to eat it

5. Find all the gazillion pieces of all the gazillion toys and put them away neatly

6. Maintain the entire family's social calendar

7. Brush the kids' teeth twice daily with natural toothpaste

8. Create perfect birthday parties with perfect goodie bags

9. Vet all service providers—doctors, babysitters, teachers

10. Conceal all mood fluctuations from . . . everybody

11. Recompose self and children to not look desperate when husband gets home

12. Arrive home from work with loads of energy for the kids

Clearly, not everything on this to-do list is doable, nor should it be. So how can we get ourselves out of this craziness and be happy raising our kids? The key is to reexamine our priorities and redefine motherhood as something we both can and want to do.

Expectations

Sorting through the thicket of our expectations is difficult but necessary. We all have expectations that we think come from other people but that really come from ourselves, and expectations from ourselves that we think are from other people. Worst of all, we not only try to meet and exceed these expectations, but we feel guilty when we don't. Take a moment to look at the following list of expectations and check off as many boxes as you feel apply to you.

- ☐ Be a good mom.
- ☐ Prove to husband that I'm a good mom.
- ☐ Go back to work ASAP.
- ☐ Go back to work after spending a year or two with kids.
- ☐ Stay home and not go back to work.
- ☐ Raise kids to be as perfect as possible.
- ☐ Have smart kids.
- ☐ Make sure kids have good manners.
- ☐ Have fresh flowers in the house.
- ☐ Be the kind of mother my mom wants me to be.
- ☐ Be the kind of mother my mom was.
- ☐ Feel lucky for all my options.

- ☐ Have regular sex with husband.
- ☐ Be the person I was before kids.
- ☐ Make gifts for Father's Day.
- ☐ Deal with most, if not all, baby duties.
- ☐ Plan activities, classes, and playdates.
- ☐ Achieve balance.
- ☐ Have well-adjusted, socialized kids.
- ☐ Look healthy and fit.
- ☐ Look sexy.
- ☐ Be happy or look happy.
- ☐ Feel fulfilled.
- ☐ Be admired.
- ☐ Have it all.
- ☐ Spend quality time with kids.
- ☐ Spearhead household chores.

- [ ] Make all doctor and dentist appointments.
- [ ] Garden.
- [ ] Maintain car.
- [ ] Oversee homework, go to conferences, and keep up on school activities.
- [ ] Buy birthday presents.
- [ ] Organize birthday parties.
- [ ] Write thank-you notes.
- [ ] Decorate for holidays.
- [ ] Buy kids' clothing and shoes.
- [ ] Pay bills.
- [ ] Throw dinner and holiday parties.
- [ ] Fix household things.
- [ ] Bathe kids.
- [ ] Brush kids' teeth.
- [ ] Put kids to bed.
- [ ] Arrange and manage child care.
- [ ] Pick up kids from school.
- [ ] Manage family relationships and gatherings.
- [ ] Take care of pet.
- [ ] Make sure grandparents regularly see kids.
- [ ] Help friends with relationship problems.
- [ ] Keep the house in order for drop-in friends and guests.
- [ ] Help friends out with their kids.

OK, now that it's all down in black-and-white, look at what's expected of you. Is it attainable? The first time we did this exercise ourselves, we didn't know if we should laugh or cry. (We did both.) But once we recomposed ourselves, one thing was absolutely clear: Our expectations were totally, completely out of whack.

6 easy pieces

You can realign your priorities—and thus your life—by following the six easy steps below. But first, take a hard look at your list of expectations, and cross off those things that really, really don't need to be there. Next, reprioritize what's on your list. Do you really *need* to have fresh flowers in the house? Do you have to drive for *every* field trip? Is hosting your moms' group for breakfast really necessary? These things are all great, but when these small expectations start becoming priorities, you can lose sight of the bigger, more important picture. At first this will feel impossible. In time it will feel liberating. Follow your instincts and your core values. The goal is to end up with only those expectations that are truly vital to your family.

1. Make a list of all the core expectations that you have of yourself and that others have of you. Pinpoint where each expectation comes from. (See list on preceding pages.)

2. Set aside anything you absolutely can't control (e.g., the need to work). These are the givens, whatever they may be, so stop worrying about them.

3. Now, looking at your list, ask yourself these questions:
   - Which of my expectations are elective?
   - If I could eliminate one pressure in my day, what would it be?
   - If I had one more hour in my day, how would I spend it?

for realigning your life

4. Go through your list again and identify your lowest priorities. For some people, keeping the house clean or putting dinner on the table is mission critical; for others, letting go of that pressure allows time to work out or do something higher on their priority list.

5. Rethink your notion of things you can't change. Is it really impossible to hire a sitter? Must you spend twenty minutes cleaning up toys five times a day?

6. Finally, tell yourself it's only a trial. Imagine you're dropping some expectations for only a week. If you want to go back to baking cupcakes from scratch next week, go right ahead.

CHAPTER 3

YOU CAN HAVE IT ALL. JUST NOT ALL AT ONCE

◦ ◦ ◦

(Make Peace With Your Choices)

quiz no. 3

WHICH OF THE FOLLOWING ARE YOU UNRESOLVED ABOUT?

CHECK ALL THAT APPLY.

- [ ] Work/stay home

- [ ] Organic/not organic

- [ ] TV/no TV

- [ ] One kid/two kids/three kids

- [ ] Music class/gymnastics class/no class

- [ ] Make kids' beds/make kids make own beds

- [ ] Bribes/punishment

- [ ] Dog/cat/fish/no pet

- [ ] Barbies or guns/no Barbies or guns

- [ ] Potty-train at two/potty-train at three

- [ ] Help kids with homework/make kids do homework themselves

- [ ] Keep kids clean/let kids run wild

WE'VE ALL BEEN THERE, OR CLOSE TO IT: SITTING ON THE BENCH, watching Billy in swim class, when the spirals of self-doubt start swirling in your head. Is this the best swim class or should he really be at La Petite Baleen? Or what about karate—should I have signed him up for karate instead? That would really help with his hand-eye coordination, but maybe he'd become a brute around the house. Should we be encouraging him to start being manly at age four? Is banning all violent toys setting him up to be a sissy for life?

If you let your mind start wandering down a road like this—and lord knows many of us have—pretty soon you'll feel like your entire life is unraveling, or like it might if you don't get your self-confidence back under control. For many mothers we talked to, questioning one choice often led to questioning another. And another. And another after that.

It's maddening. Because normally we're relatively sane. We don't go through these loops of indecision when making plans to, say, go on a bike ride or buy an anniversary gift. We're not constantly wondering if we've married the right guy (occasionally) or if we should repaint the house. But there are just so many choices and options when it comes to our children. And these are our kids, right? Even the smallest decisions matter. We want the best for them, on matters big and small. We want them to feel good about themselves, and we want them to feel good about us.

One mom we know regularly grills her three-year-old on what the other kids get for lunch at *preschool*. "Like, the kids who have the really good lunches, what do they have?" This is a competent, confident professional adult who trusts her own counsel on matters ranging from refinancing a home loan to selecting a cocktail dress. But peanut butter and banana sandwich versus macaroni and cheese? Her faith in her own instincts goes down the tube.

Part of what trips us up is that our kids, God bless them, are so impressionable and so emotional. We mean, really: If the wrong sticker or the wrong flavor of Popsicle can produce a Chernobyl-style meltdown, what's a mom to think about the consequences of choosing the wrong doctor, wrong nanny, or wrong school?

IF I COULD MAKE THE RIGHT CHOICES, MY LIFE WOULD JUST *CLICK*

Some of you may be hyperventilating. We're hyperventilating, too. We have choices everywhere, in all parts of life, and they all seem important. It's as if our whole society has been seduced by the idea that more choices mean more freedom. And as anybody who's spent any time channel surfing with DirecTV knows, this is not really true. More choices are good, sure, but only if you've done your homework. Only if you've received good advance information. Only if you know ahead of time what you actually want. Otherwise, the choices leave us antsy, unsatisfied, and confused. We think, "Is this all there is? Isn't there something better out there? How do I know if my choice is the right one?"

To feel good about the choices you make, you need to have an accurate picture of the situation you'll be in. And an accurate picture of motherhood? *Hah!* When we went into labor, we may have had diapers stacked to the ceiling and spreadsheets of household finances, but we did not have an accurate picture of how our lives would change.

The truth is, the parenting choices start even before our babies are born—what kind of birth does a mother want to have? What will she name her kid? We choose exactly when to have our kids. We even have choices about things we don't really have any choice about, like if we want to know ahead of time whether we'll have a boy or a girl. This sets up the false expectation that somehow we'll be able to plan—that is, control—the way we're mothers. We start to think (insanely) that if we could just make all the right choices, everything would turn out precisely as we'd imagined—perfect, beautiful, effortless, and great.

In fifteen years, will it be OK? Should I have done Latin or football? What will happen later? It's those choices that I wonder about. "We better start him in tennis in preschool, or else he won't be competitive later."

Maryann / 2 children, San Rafael, CA

This level of pressure is enough to send some women into the fetal position themselves, rocking back and forth. Couple this with the "you can have it all" mentality, and many more of us crumple. Because choice seems like a great thing, and it is to a point, but it's also overwhelming. All the more so if a mom starts to think of choice-making as some sort of combination lock: "If I could just make the right choices from these million options, my life would start fitting together perfectly and everything about my children and my life would just *click*."

This is not just our opinion. And this does not pertain just to moms. According to Barry Schwartz, author of *Paradox of Choice:*

> *Researchers have found that as choices proliferate past a certain point, people tend to get overloaded. They have increasing difficulty making decisions and end up less*

DIRTY LITTLE SECRET

I had a very vivid, very sexual dream about my contractor. So I fired him.

satisfied with the choices they do make. They are likely to experience regret over their choices, even those that turn out well, because they can easily imagine that other options may have turned out better. They develop unrealistically high expectations about the results of their decisions, and when decisions disappoint, as they almost always do because of those high expectations, they blame themselves. All of this can result in stress, anxiety, and unhappiness.

Got that, sister? Stress, anxiety, and unhappiness. Too many choices, more difficulty making decisions, less satisfaction with decisions made.

Too many choices tend to make us feel paralyzed. This is all the more unnerving because choice is supposed to make us feel empowered. Choice is supposed to make us free. Choice is supposed to give us control.

THE OVERWHELMING, CRUSHING RESPONSIBILITY OF IT ALL

Every mother knows she needs to pick her battles. Will the kids be clean or will they be on time? Will they watch videos or will the house be a wreck? Within a marriage, battles are often waged over daily chores. Who will give the kids their baths at night? Who will do the dishes?

With our spouses these skirmishes, while important, are often the secondary issue, not the real reason we feel burdened, not the real reason Mom is so desperate for Dad to start chipping in. As is so frequently the case, the thing we're *not* arguing about is often the real problem. And in this instance, the thing *not* being argued about is who's been charged with making decisions for the family.

Why argue over decision making? Isn't it a power and a privilege to be the one who gets to decide?

In some ways yes, but mostly no.

The truth is, making endless choices is a huge responsibility, and most of us don't even realize it. As mothers, we are often the deciders-in-chief. We make choices all day long. Choices about big things—should we work

What's the hardest choice you've had to make in motherhood?

"Figuring out the balance of my life. How much work feels right, how much babysitting feels right, how often date nights feel right, how much one-on-one time with each child feels right?"

"To stay in my marriage."

"To have a second child."

"To let my kids make their own mistakes."

"Putting my own goals on the back burner."

"To choose not to breast-feed."

"To miss my daughter's first day of school due to a work obligation."

"I have felt torn over enforcing our values when they differ from the mainstream's, resulting in my son feeling different from all his friends and left out as a result."

"To send my son to a special-needs school."

"To adopt a child."

"To live so far away from my parents and in-laws."

or stay home with the kids? Should they attend public or private school? Choices about small things—what should we make for dinner? What should be Brandon's birthday present? How many peas does Lauren need to eat? And choices about everything in between.

The trouble with this is not that it takes so much time, though it does do that, too. The trouble is that it uses up so much of our emotional and mental reserves. If a mother is the household choice-maker, her brain is constantly running a program in the background (while she's grocery shopping, doing laundry, supposedly working), trying to evaluate if the choices she's making for her family are working out as well as the choices other parents are making for theirs. Studies have shown that couples divide all sorts of mental tasks without even realizing it—who knows which phone numbers, who remembers to put the garbage out on Wednesday nights. And, chances are, the mother in any given family is the one who's charged with worrying if Megan's babysitter is spending enough time reading to her, if Miles' teacher appreciates his brilliance enough, if "kindergym" is really the best use of anyone's time. And if a mother has considered lots of options about nannies and schools and exercise classes, she will likely spend even more time worrying about these things. *Shouldn't I be looking for another sitter? Wouldn't Miles excel more in a different environment? But would it be really hard on him to switch?*

This erodes the balance and good will in a home. "Here's my take," says author Schwartz. "There's been a lot of attention paid to the amount of work women do in the household. But it's not really equal. I think what hasn't been focused on is the emotional and mental work—namely, who makes the decisions. To me this is incredibly important. Even if the husband's around and shares the kid workload, who's making the decisions about playdates, schools? The overwhelming, crushing responsibility of it all still lies with the mother. It's a false sense of being 'equals.'"

Consider the magnitude of choice-making in a typical family's life. Here is a partial list of categories about which a typical parent must make some kind of choice:

- Bedtimes
- Social activities
- Meals
- Work/not work
- Clothing
- Toys
- Health care
- Discipline
- School
- Day care
- TV
- Treats

Seem manageable? Fine. Now multiply all those categories by the various constituencies a parent is trying to please:

- Each child
- Spouse
- Bank account
- Reputation
- Friends
- Extended family
- Self

Now add another axis—time:

- Does the choice suit my family's happiness right now?
- Will it be bad in the short term but help attain goals in the coming weeks, months, and years?

If a person tried to plot all this out and write an algorithm by which to make decisions rationally, it would require some seriously advanced math.

Part of what's so exasperating is that the pressure doesn't seem to stop once a choice has been made. Making the choice is just the beginning, because immediately upon making it, we often feel the need to start validating that we've made the right one. The burden of this is not to be underestimated. The need to validate, to prove our parenting competence (if not genius), is both pervasive and destabilizing. A little bragging about how great our children are is one thing, but crowing about the perfect choices we have made for our children is another matter entirely. The former stems from love, the latter from insecurity and a need for approval. To varying degrees, this need for approval is what's driving so many women crazy. It's also leading us to turn motherhood into a profession and to overproduce our kids.

Sometimes you just have to trust the universe that things will turn out OK.

Amy / 2 children, Corte Madera, CA

We heard this again and again from mothers like Monica in Los Angeles. "After I quit my job to become a stay-at-home mother, I found myself fixating on things like my daughter's school. Her kindergarten class was called 'Chickadees,' so for the first day of school, I scoured the stores and found these Beanie Babies chickadees. I was sitting there, sweating, at eleven at night, wrapping ribbon around the chickadees with personalized medallions, and my mom looked at me and said, 'Hmmm, putting your law degree to work, huh?'"

This partial insanity and need for validation crept up in our interviews no matter where a woman sat on the work/stay-at-home divide. If a mother wasn't bringing in a paycheck, often she was trying to prove how valuable her "mommy" work was. If a mother held down a job outside the home, often she was trying to bend over backward to keep up with

I thought about the choice constantly, whether or not to work. I knew there were certain things I had to rule out in my decision making. I didn't want to be in an all-or-nothing situation. I didn't want to wake up in three years as a woman who didn't know her family. I ruled out consulting due to the travel schedule. I wasn't confident about what I did want to do; I just knew what I didn't want to do.

JOANNE / 1 CHILD, BOSTON, MA

the stay-at-home moms. For many mothers, the need to prove the sound-ness of their choices—not just to themselves, but to their spouses, to other mothers, and even to their kids—was undercutting their self-confidence and quality of life. For instance, one mother told us, "I'm constantly feeling like I'm questioning my choices. I think that the family pressure is immense—the pressure to be a good mother and a good wife. I feel like a hamster on a wheel. I get one thing off my plate and then there's another. The pressures and the questions are endless: What is this parent doing? Am I doing the wrong things? Are my children overscheduled? I'm constantly questioning my choices and feeling like I'm making the wrong ones."

I DON'T DO THAT! *SHOULD* I DO THAT?

Part of what's so hard about feeling one has made the right choices is that day-to-day life with young children is so variable. This inconsistency, coupled with the sheer volume of choices, makes a lot of mothers feel like they're never able to get into a groove. One day is pure bliss—everything's clicking, the children are angels, the routine really works. And the next day it all goes haywire—the whole family's cranky, the children have hair-trigger tempers, and Mom's a disheveled mess. As we heard repeatedly from mothers, this is when the self-doubt creeps in—thoughts like, *Are strangers staring at me? What am I doing wrong here? Am I a terrible mom?*

"I go through questioning whether this is the right choice—to stay at home—all the time," says Sonya. "I felt like I had to leave my job. It really came down to my hours and my responsibilities. But I still question it all the time: Could I have had a better balance when I worked? Could I go back and do it now?"

DIRTY LITTLE SECRET

If I'm having a crazy day, and I find myself talking to someone on the cell phone, I'll sometimes just hang up on her and pretend it was bad reception.

Another fallout from all these choices is that they put us in a reactive state instead of a proactive one. It's counterintuitive: One would think all these options would really allow mothers to get strong grips on their own lives, and make deliberate decisions about their own existences and those of their kids. But when what works one week bombs the next, choices must be remade constantly. Reevaluation and choice-making become a way of life. Mothers grow accustomed to looking over their shoulders, comparing, wondering if someone else is outmothering them.

Do not take everything that everybody says to you to heart. Is so-and-so sleeping through the night yet? Is she still drinking from a bottle? I just ran into this mother who's upset because people are giving her a hard time because her son's sleeping in her bed. I said to just put horse blinders on. That stuff will eat you up and consume your thoughts.

Rachel / 2 children, New York, NY

This comparing is a major reason that mothers feel competitive and that they need to put on a happy face. For better or worse—usually worse—many of us get caught in a trap. We think, "She looks so great/calm/happy, and her kid seems so well adjusted/healthy/smart. What's she doing? Is her choice better? Should I be doing that?"

We heard a lot of women at loose ends over fairly insignificant details. Like Debi, who told us, "When my kids go to a friend's house and they come home with crafts projects, I panic and think, 'I don't do that! *Should* I do that?' Sometimes I have to call a friend who will confirm that what I'm doing—or not doing—is fine. Sometimes I just need to take a break and get perspective that I can't do it all."

When we got married, we both thought we'd have at least three children. I recently sat down with my husband, and we decided that we are not going to have any more kids. It was hard to realize that two is our limit. So many of my friends are having three and four kids, and I'm like, "Why is three the new two?" We decided that we just love each other too much to have another baby. Since we've made that choice, it's relieved so much pressure.

Annie / 2 children, Miami, FL

EXPECTATIONS: HERE WE GO AGAIN

We heard from a lot of mothers that they crave confidence and stability. They want to stop looking over their shoulders, stop living with doubt, and stop making choices based on others' expectations of them. This reactive, comparative state leads to other problems, like a temptation to overschedule. We don't want to miss anything, right? As a result, our days get frantic. Whole lives get set up to multitask. A mother winds up with a car that doubles as a living room and makes so many casual friends she can barely keep up with the people she really cares about. Her life becomes busy. Busy, busy, busy. And this is supposed to be good.

But busy has some serious downsides. Busy can mean that although a mom thinks she's making lots of good choices, she's actually failed to prioritize. Busy can easily start to feel crazy. In a very real sense, a too-busy mom has failed to make conscious choices at all.

DIRTY LITTLE SECRET

There are times I wonder why I had kids at all. I'm not sure why I'm doing it. I worry that I don't have time to help them grow in all the ways I'd like them to grow.

6 easy steps

for making peace with your choices

As one mom in Boston told us, "I finally realized you can have it all, just not all at once." In other words, you can't do everything right now. As you've doubtless been telling your own children (or will be telling them soon), you need to learn how to make good choices for yourself and accept them. The six steps that follow will help you achieve that goal.

1. Realize that expectations can influence your choices. Make sure you're making conscious choices based on what you really want, not what is expected of you.

2. Consider what you *don't* want. By eliminating what is *not* right, what *is* right becomes clear.

3. Go back to your core principles and values. Use these to drive your choices.

4. Consider why you're feeling overloaded. It may not be just one big thing; all of those little things can add up to chaos. Making a few small changes might bring big relief.

5. Let go of the pressure to do it all and to do it all perfectly. Sometimes, it's OK for things to be "good enough."

6. Once you make a choice, make a rule not to second-guess yourself. Deciding to make peace with your choices will help keep you from being so swayed by others (and yourself).

CHAPTER 4

AM I A BAD MOM IF I DON'T BUY ORGANIC SPAGHETTIOS?

○ ○ ○

(Lose the Judgment)

quiz ^{no.}4

**RANK THESE QUESTIONS
IN ORDER OF BITCHINESS.**

___ You let your kids watch a whole movie on a school night?

___ You've got twenty hours of help a week? Aren't you a stay-at-home mom?

___ Is your daughter still in Pull-Ups?

___ Oh, you stopped breast-feeding?

___ You didn't make it to Jake's soccer game? Was he really bummed?

___ How do you guys manage to take so many date nights for yourselves? Don't you feel selfish?

___ Have you asked your kids' dentist about all the candy they eat?

___ Oh, you let your babysitter pick your kids up from school?

___ Do your kids feel cramped sharing a room?

___ That's so cute—he has Spider-Man shoes and a Spider-Man lunch box. Does he watch a lot of TV?

C'MON, WE ALL KNOW WE'VE DONE IT: SAT ON THE COUCH OR behind the steering wheel and thought, I would never do *that*. I would never let my kids eat in front of the TV; I would never let my kids watch TV, *period*; I would never let the nanny put them to bed; I would never waste my time with all those ridiculous classes; I would never let my child whine her way into getting a treat; I would never let my child stay up too late. And then we have a second (or third) child, or we go back to work, or our spouse starts working longer hours, or we just get too damn tired, and there we are, along with the rest of the moms in the trenches, doing the very things we judged them for not so very long ago.

First off, mothers *do* judge each other. Even if they don't say it, they are thinking it. Every mother thinks that she is doing it the right way, and if someone else is doing it differently, that's wrong. I know this because I've heard moms talking, and I'm guilty myself. I don't usually say anything to the other moms, but in my mind, I've already made an assumption of what kind of mother that one is, how much she loves her children, and even how her children are going to turn out! It's bad, I know.

Elissa / 2 children, Austin, TX

Most of the time we judge another person's actions not because they're truly horrible, but because they are different from ours. In other words, we judge to validate our own choices. Judging others convinces us that we're valuable and important, and that we're doing a really good job.

Judgment can also turn the envy we might feel for other mothers on its head. One minute we think, Oh, God, what would I give not to work and to have a nanny and a great car and time to spend with friends, like that woman does? The next minute we think that same mom is the worst person ever for spending three hours a day away from her children while she does the family errands and goes to the gym. And then we have to confront the fact that we, too, are just human, and our seven-year-old's idea of heaven is an afternoon alone playing computer games.

I have a "good-mom" chart in my head. I keep tally on the "good-mom" points. For instance, you can get a manicure in the afternoon, but only if you put in a certain amount of time with the kids in the morning.

Olivia / 3 children, Seattle, WA

I GO OUT OF MY WAY TO SEEM LIKE I'M NOT WORKING

Before we move on to how to minimize judgment, it's worth taking a look at some of the deeper reasons why we judge at all. We judge because it encourages conformity ("if Supermom does it like that, then I should, too") and discourages plurality ("that mother who does something different from me is a bad mom"). From this point of view, it's easy to see that judgment is good for nobody. Judgment divides us from one another and, more often than not, makes us feel bad about ourselves. It discourages us from living the particular life that would work best for us. It squelches creativity, flexibility, and individuality, three qualities we mothers so vitally need.

We don't even realize how influenced we are by the judgments, both real and perceived, that others have of us. This issue comes up a lot around working versus staying at home. When mothers choose not to go along with their families' expectations, they tend to pay a price—feeling judged. For instance, says Sherry, "With [my husband's] family, I've always felt judged. His sisters are stay-at-home moms, and they always talk about how important it is for moms to stay home to raise their kids and how it makes a big difference in how the kids turn out. Even though that's not my choice or who I am, I want them to think I'm doing a good job. So, I go out of my way to make it seem like I'm home and not working. 'Oh, here I am baking cookies! I'm the happy homemaker!'"

IF I HAVE THREE KIDS, WILL I LOOK LIKE A SUCCESSFUL MOM?

One reason we compare and judge is the fact that life has changed for many people in the last generation or two, and most of us can't look to our own mothers as role models. For instance, one of the first things we were all supposed to do when our children were born—namely, nurse them—was a totally foreign experience to most of our own moms. And it wasn't entirely intuitive either. So there we were, with still-wrinkled newborns in our arms, and we started looking to friends and neighbors for help. Which was great and all—how on earth were we supposed to figure out how to get that baby to latch on?—but it set a precedent: *Look around at what others are doing.* Many of us have become somewhat programmed to first look at what other moms are doing and then compare ourselves to that. While this approach works well for universal things like breast-feeding or swaddling a baby, when it comes to bigger

DIRTY LITTLE SECRET

I lost my toddler when she was one, and a stranger found her riding up and down on the elevator by herself.

The Comeback Chart

We know we should be "above it all," but every now and then, we just need to blurt out a good comeback when we feel judged. Here are some to rehearse.

SCENARIO	COMEBACK
Your toddler is still in a crib?	Of course! The latest research proves that the longer you keep them in cribs, the smarter they are.
Can he say his ABCs yet?	No, but he can swear in five languages. Wanna hear?
You let her watch TV?	Oh, yeah. And her favorite movie is *The Exorcist*. She can perfectly imitate the Linda Blair character. You've got to come over and see it.
Does your husband help you with the housework?	No, I just keep him locked in the bedroom, where he belongs. He's my sex slave.
What do you do all day?	You know what? Absolutely nothing. Nada. I sit on my booty and eat bonbons and watch a little *All My Children* if I've got the energy. How about you?
Were your twins conceived naturally?	Oh, yes. They were conceived doggy-style.

choices, like choosing a school for our child, we really need to focus on what specifically is right for our families.

Some women are lucky enough to have sisters and friends who live nearby to see them through the rough spots. More than money, more than power, even more than sex, living close to our dearest friends and being able to barge in and drop off the kids without asking first—knowing full well that when it's needed in return, the same will be asked of us—is something we've heard moms desperately crave. But the reality for most of them is pretty different—they live in cities they didn't grow up in, with friends they've made in the past two or five or ten years. Their support systems are newer and more tentative. They've worked hard to build them, and had to jettison a lot of often judgmental "friends" along the way.

I've only talked to a few moms about this. I find that these conversations don't take place very often. It's a vulnerable position, to admit that you find that you're falling short on motherhood's side, and you're speaking with someone who in your mind has complete success with it.

Meredith / 2 children, Mill Valley, CA

If we're smart about building our support systems, we'd search for fellow moms who didn't judge us for being different, needy, or imperfect. We'd seek out women who could give us good advice without making us feel bullied or dumb. These traits are especially important because, unlike breast-feeding, most mothering chores aren't universal and thus aren't well suited to a conformist mindset. And if we're still caught up in this mindset when our kids hit preschool, we're sunk. Because we'll start thinking we need to do everything the other mothers do. And we'll get competitive. And then we'll do things that aren't right for us. One mom even said to us, amazingly, "I decided to have three kids because as a stay-at-home mother I thought it would make me look like a more successful mom. But, sadly, no one cared."

Most of the time, of course, mothers choose simpler methods of validation, but the mechanism is the same: looking for it outside, not developing it inside. There we are in our sweatpants, sitting in the sandbox or dropping the kids off at school, observing the moms who are working, dressed perfectly, and doing PTA, and we compare ourselves to them. As a result, we wind up (a) pitting ourselves against an image and (b) trying to compete with that image, perhaps by doing way too much, just because we feel like we should.

Sounds silly, but we've been there. We've worn the sweatpants, and we know. We've signed up for classes because we thought they'd make us better mothers. We've cooked scrambled tofu. We've bought flash cards. We've volunteered to be class mom. We've called in sick to work to stuff goodie bags. We realized at the time that it was a bit ridiculous, but even moms who know that this behavior is over-the-top have a hard time resisting it. As one mother, Krista, from Pennsylvania, told us, "Now that we're entering preschool, I feel like I'm back in high school. The peer pressure is immense. You want to get friendly with other moms so your child is included in playdates and gatherings, and to some extent that responsibility lies with the mother. I'm not into that at all! I thought I was done with those politics in high school!"

SUPERMOM HAS ISSUES, TOO

A big issue for a lot of us is the idea that we're supposed to be perfect moms. We're supposed to go to every soccer game, nurture every tiny talent, and never raise our voices. But when we (again) fail to meet our expectations, or when other mothers fail to meet our expectations, that's where the judgment starts.

We all can admit that we've unjustly judged another mom, especially if we haven't experienced what the other mother is experiencing. Yet in the end we only feel crazier and more out-of-control if we hang on to the idea that we can do it all, and do it all perfectly. We all supposedly let go of that

The only reason why I signed my son up for this preschool-preparation class was that all the moms in my moms' group convinced me that he'd be up to speed faster and his skills would be sharper. It's not how I really wanted to spend my time with him, but I wasn't confident enough to opt out.

AMANDA / 2 CHILDREN, DETROIT, MI

I'm not a continual keeping-up-with-the-Joneses kind of mom, but you can't help but be influenced by how your friends are doing things. Nicole is right on target for her age, but still I think I should be doing flash cards and helping out in a more direct way. A lot of that comes from my girlfriend who homeschools. Her son is just a whiz at math.

SARAH / 2 CHILDREN, LOS ANGELES, CA

1980s vision of the supermom years ago, but the truth is, that didn't really happen. Supermom, or at least her myth, is alive and well. "That's the secret," one mom told us. "The real 'superachiever' moms just don't sleep. They get three extra hours per day!"

Many of us planned when we wanted to become parents, sometimes right down to the month, and this gave us a false sense that motherhood was something we could control. Needless to say, if you have children, you've probably got a good sense that you won't be controlling your life in motherhood anytime soon. And trying to won't make you any happier, either. A better sense of control, oddly, comes from letting go. You can't always control your child's mood. You can't ensure they'll be good swimmers. As one mom said, "I had an epiphany when my pediatrician told me that it's my job to provide the resources for my kids, but I can't always control the outcome—like if they eat the food I prepare."

I had a huge fear of being judged when I was deciding whether to quit my job. I thought, "How will I be perceived? Will this look like a cop-out? What will my friends think?"

Kelly / 2 children, Fairfield, CT

Doing more—more classes, more flash cards—simply doesn't guarantee how our kids will turn out. Yes, we too would like to have children who both win Nobel Prizes and score the winning goal in the World Cup, but that probably isn't going to happen, and we should stop pretending that whether it does is some kind of reflection on our skills as parents. Yes, we need to give our children food, shelter, health care, education, and tons of

DIRTY LITTLE SECRET

I forgot to strap my newborn daughter in her car seat. When I got home, she just kind of fell out.

love. But thinking our kids are what we make them is not only pointless but crushes their individuality, stresses them out, and screws everybody up.

WHILE I WAS SAUTÉING ONIONS, MY BABY CONSUMED SIX CRAYONS

So we judge both ourselves and others. And what happens when we do? We label ourselves "bad moms." This judgment/bad-mom cycle happens far too quickly and too frequently.

Concepts of the idealized mom and how she should behave bombard us from all angles. Helena describes a fairly typical moment. "I was watching a morning show, and there was a segment on how the latest research shows that watching videos is hugely detrimental to our kids' brains and how they'll function as adults. The pediatric experts were going on and on about how parents today don't realize that even twenty minutes of Elmo a day could damage a child. I broke into a cold sweat and immediately questioned whether I was a bad mom."

I had one friend who went back to work right after having a baby. I felt like, C'mon, at least take your maternity leave. I *did* judge her! She's a bad mother! In the meantime, I was just really jealous.

Anonymous / 2 children, New York, NY

Another key trigger that makes a lot of us feel like bad moms is the problem of eating dinner together, as a family. Many of us grew up in families where everyone sat down together for a meal every night. This is wonderful, but sometimes, even if we've had the best day, when we can't sit down together for dinner, we feel like we've failed. For some people, a family dinner is and should remain a top priority. As one mom told us, "I had to talk to my boss and get permission to come in earlier and leave earlier so I could come home for dinner. Sometimes it's takeout and sometimes it's a frozen pizza—but I realized for our family it had to be a priority."

One thing I've learned over the years is that when you become a mother, you become a mother to everybody's children. And it doesn't matter whose kids they are. We all have an obligation to help the other moms. I cannot tell you how many strangers were so kind to me in helping me raise my children. I've had people who emptied my groceries into my car. And I will do that today. Just help each other; that's what we need to do.

JENNIFER / 5 CHILDREN, DETROIT, MI

But it's worth considering whether this is the case for you. Young children may be hungry before your partner is home (or may not care for the salmon you're slaving over), and suddenly, the family dinner becomes an extremely stressful and inconvenient concept. A good question to ask yourself is what you're hoping to get out of the meal. Good food is great, and nutrition is important, but the real goal for many of us is quality family time. Perhaps your family's quality time comes after everyone is fed, hanging out in the backyard. And that's OK, too.

It's really hard for me to get dinner on the table, especially when I work. In the ten minutes that I was sautéing onions and browning the meat, my baby consumed six crayons. Are they toxic? I was on the phone with Poison Control. It's horrible—my husband and I almost broke up over dinner; it's a sore spot for us. I just have to let go and accept less than perfection.

Karen / 2 children, Pittsburgh, PA

Depending on the communities we live in, we feel different pressures concerning the kinds of mothers we're supposed to be. In some areas, women feel they need to do it all themselves—or at least give that appearance. "I have four kids between the ages of two and ten," one mom told us. "And not one of my friends has even one hour of child-care help. I'm afraid that if I were to hire a babysitter for even a few hours a week, they would look at me like a failure or a cop-out. So I do it to myself. I'm stretched way beyond my limits, and I don't have one second to myself, ever, but I guess that's better than the alternative."

In other areas, the pressures are exactly the opposite. For instance, many urban mothers spoke to us about the pressure to have "meaningful" work. Said one mom, "Where we live, it's such a close community. I think maybe I'll be judged or my husband will be judged or my kids will be judged if I don't go back to work. I thought I'd have much more openness about it."

Of course, when it comes to other people, it's very easy to say *stop judging!* The great thinkers of the world have been telling us to do this since time immemorial. "Maybe we all need to recognize that there are many ways to be a 'good mother,'" Jan, from Boston, wisely told us. "There's no one magical 'right' path. Realizing this has really helped me. For instance, just because one mom is disciplining her child differently than I would doesn't make her a 'bad' mom, just different. And that should be OK. I don't take it personally now either when I feel someone is judging me."

I started realizing how much I actually judge other moms. My sister homeschools her kids, and I would always silently criticize her choices. Once I became aware of it, I started to realize how it only made me feel worse in the end. Now I stop myself and instead think, "Hey, if it works for them, great. Maybe they know something I don't." And now I find myself speaking up in my circle of friends if I hear someone else saying something judgmental. Motherhood is hard enough without this pressure, too.

Amelia / 2 children, Detroit, MI

IF YOU SHOW UP WITH A SPECK OF MASCARA, I'LL BE PISSED!

How to combat judgment? The most important thing you can do is to build a real support network for yourself. And when talking to moms, we heard repeatedly that the key to finding real support is to be open and honest. We're not suggesting you start telling your gory labor stories to every woman with a toddler you see in the grocery checkout line. But we

DIRTY LITTLE SECRET

I let my six-year-old watch *Access Hollywood* with me.

are suggesting that when you talk to fellow parents about your lives in motherhood, you start telling the truth.

If you haven't yet built a support group for yourself, one thing to consider is whether you're being honest. If you're still committed to maintaining an illusion that your life is perfect, those around you probably think you don't need any help or wouldn't be receptive to hearing about the thousand ways they're bumbling through their days. Those women who say everything is great, great, great drive us crazy, not only because they make us feel bad about ourselves, but because—pardon our language—we think they're full of crap. One mother, Meg, described for us how she became a pretty tough customer in terms of picking friends. "I don't have the desire or patience or time for 'pleasant' friendships with women anymore," she told us. "Sounds mean, but I expect more from friends now—no crap."

Our generation of moms feel like they have to be perfect. When I have conversations with my mom, she'll say, "Getting angry happened weekly, if not daily, when I was a mom, and you're not scarred, are you? You have this vision of being so perfect, but you are *human*, and you need them to understand that you make mistakes, so they realize that it's OK to make mistakes too."

Krista / 2 children, Yardley, PA

Another mom told us about an agreement she has with her friends. "I actually have a pact I make with certain friends when they come over. They are *not* allowed to wear a stitch of makeup, they have to wear sweats, and there is no judgment allowed. I don't judge your messy house, and you don't judge mine. I'll say, 'I'm dead serious—if you show up with a speck of mascara, I'll be pissed!'"

I recently realized that I can't be everything to everybody. I have had to remove myself from playgroups that make me feel bad. There is judgment for staying home, and other mothers judge me for the choices I make in my day-to-day life. Why do we need to compete? It makes everyone feel bad. Shouldn't we help each other?

KELLY / 2 CHILDREN, FAIRFIELD, CT

The best advice was from myself: There's not one right way to do things. The people who are the most judgmental are the ones who aren't comfortable with the choices they've made. I've come to learn this, and it makes me a less judgmental person on a day-to-day basis.

LINDSAY / 2 CHILDREN, BOSTON, MA

It's human nature to judge each other. But I do believe that when I'm about to judge someone, I try to look at myself and ask why I feel that way. It must be about me.

SHANNON / 2 CHILDREN, SAN FRANCISCO, CA

7 steps

to Getting a Grip on Judgment

1. Start to become aware of the moments when you negatively judge yourself.

2. Strive for your own personal best instead of 100 percent perfect.

3. Open yourself up to recognizing good-mom moments. Even the small things—like spending ten minutes of one-on-one time or reading a book together—matter.

4. When you're about to judge someone or yourself, ask why you're doing it. One mom told us that she decided to say *judge* every time she had a judgmental thought. She was surprised at how often that was.

5. If you find yourself judging someone, try to put yourself in that mom's position and look at the issue from her perspective.

6. Let go of judgments of others based on what's come to be known as "normal."

7. Make sure your support system is working for you. As one mom put it, "it's not a real moms' group unless someone's crying."

CHAPTER 5

I COUNT THE HOURS SHE SPENDS WITH THE NANNY AND MAKE SURE I HAVE MORE

. . .

(Let Go of the Guilt)

quiz ^{no.} 5

**WHICH STATEMENTS ARE TRUE
(AND YOU WISH THEY WEREN'T)?**

CHECK ALL THAT APPLY.

☐ You yell at your kids semiregularly.

☐ You look forward to going to work.

☐ You turn on Noggin so you can check your e-mail.

☐ You split a box of mac and cheese with your kids for dinner whenever your husband is out of town.

☐ You can see your bad mood reflected on your children's faces.

☐ You throw your kids at your husband when he walks in the door.

☐ You quit nursing because you felt like a cow.

☐ You let your baby scream to put herself to sleep.

☐ You throw away your kids' drawings while they're sleeping.

☐ Your kids ask, "Why are you so happy, Mommy?" when you're having a good day.

AMAZING BUT TRUE: WE HAVE A KNACK FOR FEELING GUILTY OVER almost anything related to motherhood. Really, you name it, and we've felt guilty about it. Leaving a diaper on too long, changing diapers too often. Being late to pick up a kid from a playdate, being early to pick up a kid from a playdate. Buying our children sweets, not buying our children sweets. Enforcing bedtimes, not enforcing bedtimes. Taking time to put ourselves back together, not taking time to put ourselves back together. It's quite miraculous and very destructive, this ability of ours to feel guilty. And we are not alone. Nearly every mom we talked to was feeling guilty about something. One mom summed it up: "I even feel guilty about feeling guilty!"

Why is this happening? Some would argue that we're biologically predisposed to feel guilt. (Erica Jong once wrote, "Show me a woman who doesn't feel guilt and I'll show you a man.") Personally, we believe our guilt comes from our inflated expectations. Every day, at least in our own heads, we fall short of the goals that we've set for ourselves. And that makes us feel bad. Each day we wake up, run around all day, and then go to sleep with an endless litany of shouldas, couldas, wouldas, and have-tos. As a result, we live in our shortcomings, in a state of constant regret.

Here is a partial list of things about which mothers told us they felt guilty:

- Not eating well enough during pregnancy
- Wanting a boy
- Wanting a girl
- Hating to change diapers
- Having only one child
- Not bonding with the second baby like they did with the first
- Neglecting to update baby books
- Going back to work
- Feeling like sex is a chore
- Not giving each child enough one-on-one time
- Failing to do enough for the holidays
- Serving prepared foods for dinner
- Not reading enough books
- Not saving enough money for children's educations
- Hiring a babysitter for too many hours
- Spoiling children by spending too much time with them
- Thinking about work while playing with the kids
- Not feeling close to stepchildren
- Failing to brush kids' teeth
- Fighting with spouse in front of children
- Nagging
- Losing their tempers
- Rushing through bedtime stories
- Feeling thrilled when the kids fall asleep

Although our guilt is pervasive, we've noticed it tends to creep up most often at particular times.

One common occasion for guilt is when *our children behave badly*. It may seem counterintuitive that *we* feel bad when *they* act badly, but we believe part of our job as moms is shaping our children into the best people they can be. So we're supposed to correct bad behavior, right? And that means correcting it firmly and now. Thus, when our children are disrespectful, or just plain mean or obnoxious, we try to shape them up, and this sometimes leads to yelling. And right on the heels of the yelling come the waves of guilt.

Another major and all-too-common time for maternal guilt is those rare moments in our days *when we stop being Mom*. Again and again, mothers told us that no matter what they might be doing—say, taking a much-needed mental-health break to have lunch with a friend—they felt guilty if they stopped tending their children or thinking about them. This is a trap, of course, because if we don't give ourselves license to be independent adults, we're guaranteed to wear out, lose our cool, and snap at our kids.

When your kids reach toddlerhood and start wising up, a whole new realm of guilt kicks in: *when our children intentionally make us feel guilty*. Nearly every mother who'd finished with diapers had a story on this theme. Sometimes it had to do with one child making a mother feel guilty over paying too much attention to a sibling. Often it would be about guilt-tripping Mom for going to work. Kids reach a certain age, and they just start pressing our buttons. "How come you have to go out again,

DIRTY LITTLE SECRET

I tell my daughter that I'll check on her in two minutes each night when I say goodnight . . . but I never do.

I feel a constant stream of guilt, always. Yesterday I was in my living room and my little twins were propped up, hanging out. It must've been fifteen or twenty minutes before I realized that Caroline had been staring at me, hoping I would catch her eye, and when I finally looked at her, she squealed with excitement. I just welled up and thought, "How awful a mom am I, that I'm not paying enough attention to my own babies?" The pressure is just intense.

KEIRA / 3 CHILDREN, MILL VALLEY, CA

Mom?" This technique is both effective and pernicious in that it usually compounds the guilt we already feel.

Transition times are also notorious for creating problems of all kinds, including maternal guilt. Getting the kids ready for school in the morning, putting the kids to bed in the evening, even getting the kids to decamp from the playground—all these can cause stress for everybody involved. And when there's stress, there are outbursts. And when there are outbursts, Mom feels bad.

Mothers must go through their own transitions, too—when we *flip the switch,* as many mothers call it—and these times produce guilt, too. Physically, mentally, and emotionally, many mothers inhabit multiple worlds, and shuttling back and forth between them can be jarring. A mother's professional persona often moves at a different speed and uses a different tone of voice than the lady kids know as Mom.

Right now I'm in the middle of it—I have a newborn. I run my own business, and I'm at the computer trying to send something on deadline, the baby is screaming and crying, and the toddler is jealous, throwing her body on the ground in a tantrum. Sometimes I just plow forward and get what I'm working on *out* and deal with the guilt afterward. Then I stop and think, Oh, my God, what am I doing? In the grand scheme of things, is this really important? Should I forget about this work stuff and concentrate on just the kids?

Sherry / 2 children, Atlantic Highlands, NJ

WHAT'S THE PROBLEM, HONEY? THEY LOVE TV

At the risk of sounding all "men are from Mars, women are from Venus," we humbly submit the notion that fathers don't have the guilt gene. We haven't located the exact chromosomal sequence or done a double-blind scientific study or anything, but we have heard the same stories again and again. Feed the kids chicken nuggets for dinner? Let them watch TV all day? Men typically don't worry much about these things. And not only do men not sweat the small stuff, but many often don't sweat things that are relatively big. Says Christopher, who works part-time from home and is the primary caregiver of two children, "Occasionally I've had to let the baby cry uncontrollably in her crib while I go out the back door to make a phone call. That's just the way it is. I don't feel guilty for that."

The limited guilt that dads do feel tends to be focused on specific circumstances and actions, not some vague notion of being a bad dad. According to the "Guilt Survey" published by Julie Bort, Aviva Pflock, and Devra Renner in their book *Mommy Guilt,* twice as many dads as moms reported no feelings of parental guilt whatsoever. And those dads who did feel guilt tended to focus it on concrete, identifiable issues (eating habits, SAT scores), while moms worried about subtleties and emotions. The result? Dads often feel frustrated as parents, but they rarely feel guilt. Yes, a father who inadvertently whacks his daughter in the head while tossing around a baseball is going to feel guilty. But he's probably not going to question his choices. He won't take the accident as a referendum on whether he's a good father.

I finally agreed to start traveling again for work when my second baby was nearly a year old. And when I got back home, she wouldn't even really look at me. She was so mad that most of my milk had dried up. We're having a huge relationship drama. She keeps dragging pillows into my lap. She can't walk or talk, but she knows how to make me feel horrible.

Liz / 2 children, San Francisco, CA

One interesting case to consider is the dad who's a parenting superhero and the effect this has on the mom's ambient guilt. We should all be so lucky as to have a spouse who pulls his weight around the house, let alone one who walks in at the end of the day with a stockpile of positive

I feel guilty when I storm in the door from work and my head isn't wrapped around the needs of two toddlers; my fuse can quickly shorten. I'm thinking, "What kind of a mom am I? I've barely been home for five minutes!"

ASHLEY / 2 CHILDREN, MINNEAPOLIS, MN

energy. But what if we look grouchy by comparison? What if we can't sustain the expectation of the parent as guardian devoted to fun? Superhero Dad begs the question, What the hell's wrong with Mom? One mother admitted to us that her husband was such a tireless father, it got her down on herself: "If my husband doesn't take time out for himself and I need to, I feel like a failure when I take a breather, and I of course feel guilty."

YOU FEEL GUILTY ABOUT *WHAT?!*

The first and most important question to ask yourself when you start feeling guilty is, Does my guilt make any sense? Guilt is supposed to be that little voice in our heads telling us that we've done something wrong. Sometimes that voice tells us something meaningful (like *Time to get in gear!*), and sometimes it doesn't know when to shut up.

But watch out for feeling guilty over every tiny thing. Isolated guilt over something very particular—say, failing to keep your word to a child—is much more likely to be justified than feeling constant guilt over every item you did (or did not do) that day. Do you worry that checking e-mail while your kids are watching videos is ruining their lives? Do you obsess over serving broccoli as a vegetable five nights in a row?

Take a deep breath, sister. Motherhood is about love, not performance. Let it go.

One good way to start letting go is to just listen, rationally, to all those crazy thoughts that are racing around in your head. Say you forgot to get your daughter a larger pair of ballet slippers. Your mind might start doing this: "Whoops! Can't believe I didn't do that! Jordon is going to get

DIRTY LITTLE SECRET

We've agreed not to have a TV in our house. The moment my husband goes out of town, I pull out the hidden thirteen-inch screen and rent some videos for my kids.

sore feet in class again, and the teacher will really wonder whether I am a fit parent. Am I a fit parent? Maybe I shouldn't be working. I'm just too busy to be a good mom. But then who would pay the bills?"

I felt horribly guilty for everything until my husband said, "Just think about how many generations of people have been completely ignored by their parents!" Most people have ignored their kids! I am not some crazy weirdo, so I've got a good chance at raising normal kids. And the truth is I am doing a pretty darn good job. If I let them watch TV all the time, they'd still be fine. So, I try to relax a little bit. We're not making or breaking them 100 percent.

Kim / 3 children, Madison, NJ

Yes, in a perfect world, you would have remembered to get the shoes. But that's no reason to think you are an unfit mother or you should quit your job. A great way to catch yourself is to ask, Is there anything I can do about it? And that's a question worth asking. We feel guilt all the time over circumstances we can't control. We feel guilty when another child snubs our child. We feel guilty when it's too cold or too rainy to go outside to play. And these are all things that are out of our control, so nip this kind of thinking in the bud, and give yourself a break.

But what about the things you think you *should* be able to control—for example, misbehaving children? We feel guilty when our children misbehave. And there are times and degrees of misbehavior for which we should all take some responsibility—say, your kid screaming during a wedding ceremony—but more often than not, we need to realize that our children are not our puppets. We do not control them. They are not entirely a reflection of ourselves. Yes, we need to teach them the basics of civil behavior, and we also need to do our best to keep them from ruining other people's good times. But—and this is a hard concept for many mothers to believe—*we are not responsible for everything our children do*. Their achievements, to a great extent, are *their* achievements. Their shortcomings are *their* shortcomings. If one of our kids has a meltdown at a dinner party, we shouldn't feel guilty about it. Stressed? Upset? Sure. Just not guilty.

In fact, there are times when we, as mothers, behave badly, and our guilt is deserved. Happens to everybody—nothing to be too ashamed about—but if you have genuinely made a mistake, it's normal to feel bad. From our own experience, and from our interviews, we've learned that these moments happen most often when we're tired and stretched too thin. Ideally, we'd keep ourselves from getting so frayed in the first place. But if we do act out, we can learn from our mistakes and avoid doing it again. As one New York City mom of two toddler boys admitted, "The only time I ever spanked my kid, we were on vacation, and my husband was working during the week. It was terrible. I grew up in a house where spanking was expected. This one time that I did it, I went into the bathroom and vomited."

It's OK to lose it. We all lose it.

Sarah / 1 child, Los Angeles, CA

Discussions about guilt inevitably lead to discussions of strange behavior. We may not all be vomiting or wringing our hands while sleepwalking like Lady Macbeth, but we're behaving bizarrely nonetheless. We heard about moms regularly lying to bosses about why they're late to work— lame excuses like a flat tire—to avoid guilt over making their children the first to arrive at day care every single day. We also heard about moms keeping their kids up till eleven at night so they'd get enough snuggles in after work. And then we heard about urban myths, like the one about the poor Catholic mom giving birth to her umpteenth child. The nurses cleaned off the baby and handed it to the mother, only to hear her say, completely delusionally, "What a beautiful baby! But why are you giving it to me? It's not mine. No, no, definitely not my child."

I started training for a marathon because I needed to do something. I feel bad that [my husband] gets home from work and I'm like, "See ya!" But everyone needs me. I feel guilty for going, sure, but I'd been putting myself last. Now if I'm having a bad day, I bitch to my girlfriend, go for a run, and I'm happier.

CHRISTY / 1 CHILD, RICHMOND, CA

While I'm PMS-ing and during my period, I erupt more. It's rough, and the guilt is overwhelming. I feel like a bad mom. I've learned that I can say to them, "You know, Mommy is having a rough day, and I'm not perfect, and I'm sorry about how I acted." Recently my son said, "You're having a rough day, huh, Mommy?" And I said, "Thank you so much for realizing that." It really helps being honest with my kids about it.

KRISTA / 2 CHILDREN, YARDLEY, PA

10 easy steps

1. Take a look at your priorities. Ask yourself if you need to do it all. You just can't keep your husband, your friends, your children, and yourself happy all the time. There's just no way.

2. Make sure you're focusing on the big things (e.g., Am I giving him enough hugs?), and let go of some of the small things that can make you crazy (e.g., Did I get him the right scooter?).

3. Ask yourself these questions:
   - Is my guilt appropriate?
   - Will I care, or will my child care, about this issue one year from now? Five years from now?
   - How does this issue fit into the overall value structure of our family?

4. Start to recognize your personal triggers. Do you have a shorter fuse if you haven't eaten lunch? Are you impatient if you've slept badly?

5. Define yourself by your best moments, not your worst. Find one thing you *did* do right today, and focus on that.

6. Figure out if your guilt is truly relevant. One mom's idea was to do this: every time you feel guilty for an action, replace the word *guilt* with *regret*. For example, "I feel guilty for going to exercise class." Do you regret going to exercise class? If not, then your guilt is unfounded.

for (almost) guilt-free mothering

7. If your guilt is founded, do what you need to do to make amends and move on. There's no benefit to beating yourself up.

8. Don't buy into others' attempts to make you feel guilty. For example, a friend might ask, "Can your kid really handle being at preschool for so many hours?" Recognize these questions for what they are: attempts to manipulate you.

9. Stick to your limits. Consistently. If your rule is that your kids get thirty minutes of TV per day, allow them thirty minutes, and don't feel guilty saying no when they ask for more. Learn to accept the fact that you are going to be responsible for many of your children's tears.

10. Realize that it's okay to have pleasure without guilt.

CHAPTER 6

JUST GIVE US A RULE BOOK. WE CAN'T BOOK. WE CAN'T READ MINDS

· · ·

(Tell Him What You Need)

quiz no. 6

YOU REALLY LOVE YOUR HUSBAND. YOU
JUST FIND IT RATHER AMAZING THAT...

CHECK ALL THAT APPLY.

- [ ] His idea of fifty-fifty is to change a diaper. Once a week.

- [ ] He can't figure out why you don't want to have sex with him every day.

- [ ] He can't flip a steak *and* watch the kids.

- [ ] He rarely says, "Thank you" or "I appreciate that you . . ."

- [ ] His idea of cleaning up the house is picking up his own shoes.

- [ ] He's sure your job is easier than his.

- [ ] He has no clue what it takes to brush the kids' teeth, get them fed, and hustle them out the door on time in the morning.

- [ ] He can rewire the stereo system, but he can't restock the diaper bag.

- [ ] He has the balls to tell you he thinks the babysitter is cute.

- [ ] He continues doing the *New York Times* crossword puzzle while surrounded by utter chaos.

- [ ] He refers to a kid with a snotty nose as "your child."

IT'S TIME TO DEVOTE A CHAPTER TO OUR MUCH-MALIGNED husbands. Thousands of books have been written about marriage, so we can't possibly hope to tackle marital problems in one single chapter. But in our continuing mission to improve our enjoyment of motherhood, and to live the fullest, happiest lives we can, we figured we should probably try to understand the men we're living with. Parenthood has not been easy on them, either.

Yes, this is a book about the challenges of being a contemporary mom. Yes, this book is devoted to helping you sort out all your conflicting roles. But our husbands, poor guys, are married to us, which can't always be a picnic. The same stuff that has us off-balance and anxious in motherhood has made fatherhood difficult for them.

As part of this effort to better understand our spouses, we talked to fathers and we heard many of the same underlying themes we heard from moms. We heard a lot about the pressure to be a good dad, to be a good husband, to be a good provider. We also heard that, like us, many fathers today feel lost as parents, as if they don't have adequate role models on which to base their lives. All this makes sense. For men, just like for women, gender roles are a lot less clear-cut than they were several decades ago. Many of our husbands' fathers didn't change a single diaper. Needless to say, this isn't a realistic or (entirely helpful) template for how most fathers today live.

A boner in the back is not foreplay.

ARLENE / 2 CHILDREN, SOUTHFIELD, MI

In thinking and talking about fatherhood today, we focused our attention on understanding their perspective and learning how what we're going through affects them. We figure those are the problems we can probably do the most about and that those are the problems we have the most responsibility to try to solve. And those problems, much to our embarrassment, are not inconsequential. Our husbands have to deal with such things as our crazy perfectionism and our ever-changing views of what "equal partnership" means. And guys, in case you're reading over your wives' shoulders, we'd also like to apologize and explain. We aren't the same women we were when we first hooked up with you. We're crankier. We have shorter fuses.

We have kids.

IT'S JUST OUR OWN CRAP

Miscommunication and the wrong kind of fantasies—OK, delusions—are major contributing factors to the stresses many, many husbands and wives feel with each other as parents. Many of the expectations we have of each other are actually just projection. We call these "imaginary expectations." For instance, some of us may think that our husbands secretly want a four-course meal on the table every evening. Or we may delude ourselves that they need us to be sex kittens in the bedroom every night. Many of us imagine that our husbands judge us for not being more productive during the day. Then, say, a husband comes home from work, opens the refrigerator, and innocently asks, "Is there any guac?" and we break down crying, beating ourselves up for not going to the market, thinking that he must be insinuating that we are not doing our job right. And it's really just our own crap. Poor guy.

DIRTY LITTLE SECRET

Whenever my husband leaves his stuff lying around, I lock it in the closet. "Have you seen my shoes?" "Have you seen my wallet?"

The truth is, we've all changed more than we might care to admit since we spruced up for our first dates, lord knows how many years ago. We may be so out of touch with ourselves and each other that we're making bad guesses about what our spouses need and want.

So an important first step toward understanding what's going on with your children's father is figuring out who that guy is. The transformation from husband and wife to father and mother profoundly impacts our identities. Priorities shift. Household psychodynamics change. A rare, lucky few of us are at our best under pressure, but most of us are testier, brittler, and more prone to crack.

LAYING DOWN EXPECTATIONS

Just as we mothers need to get a grip on the insane expectations we have of ourselves, we also need to get a grip on the expectations we have of our husbands. Parenting, as we all know, does not turn out exactly as we might have imagined. The men we're married to are fathers in their own idiosyncratic, sometimes charming, sometimes infuriating ways.

When talking with women about their husbands as fathers, we heard a lot of pleasant surprise as well as a lot of uncertainty about who those guys sharing their houses really are.

- "I thought that my husband wanted me to be a stay-at-home mom, but now it doesn't seem like we're on the same page."
- "It took a good two years for him to embrace fatherhood, and that was initially surprising and very hurtful to watch."
- "I thought he would be more disciplined with the kids."
- "My husband has suddenly become the guy who is obsessed with capturing the cute moments with our kids. His camera is glued to his hip."
- "I hoped my husband would get up in the middle of the night, or at least change a diaper, once in a while."
- "I thought he'd just be home at 6 P.M. most nights now that we have a baby, but his priorities don't seem to have changed much."

The core issue for happily parenting together is the same core issue for happily mothering by ourselves: expectations. For better or worse, we had certain expectations of our husbands going into parenthood (and they, of course, had certain expectations of us). And for better or worse, many of these expectations have not been met.

There's not a magic bullet to ease the expectations problem. Accepting reality takes time. But the most important thing we can do is explicitly discuss our expectations, the difficulty of our realities, and what we need to make our way peacefully through our all-too-real daily lives.

Just talking with each other—on a daily or even weekly basis—about how we're doing as parents and our expectations of each other can bring huge relief and pave the road for success. Do you think he expects you to stay home with the kids? Are you sure? Have you asked him? Does he know that the reason you're so pissed is that you've been waiting for him to get up with the baby in the middle of the night? One couple we know fought regularly during vacations because the husband pulled out his BlackBerry at unannounced times, making his wife want to shove it you-know-where. "Finally," she told us, "we sat down and made a rule that he could check in with work from 2 to 3 each afternoon. Just laying down that expectation changed the whole tenor of our family vacations."

I COME HOME, AND IT'S LIKE I'M THE SUBORDINATE ON PROBATION

So what do our husbands have to say for themselves?

Like us, they feel as if they're falling short, letting people down, and burning out from the tireless grind.

The truth is, in many ways our husbands' experiences are pretty similar to ours. Today's fathers, like today's mothers, are feeling overwhelming pressure—pressure to build great careers, pressure to be hands-on fathers, pressure to be emotionally supportive, pressure to pull their weight with the household chores. What's more, our husbands are feeling over-whelmed by the pressure to try to satisfy *us*. To live up to the expectations

The Bitch Session

OK, we love our husbands. But just between us girls, we've got a few issues we need to vent. Well, uh, maybe a lot of them.

Who Is This Guy and Why Is He in My House?

What we've heard is that many moms are terrified of slipping into traditional roles. The mere thought of this breeds anger and resentment toward their husbands. For instance, says Amy, "I don't mind being a mom, but when I feel even an inkling of Beaver Cleaver–land, it makes me want to run. Rationally, I know he's doing his share. But the more I give, the more I feel like my identity is shrinking."

We Don't Want to Be Fixed

Men are problem solvers. This is great when somebody needs to figure out why the garage door won't open, but we are people, tender ones, and sometimes we just want to be understood. Or heard. Or empathized with. We are not always looking for a solution. Not everything requires change. Sometimes—frequently—we just want our husbands to listen, really listen. No need to go get the nail gun.

Someone Needs to Learn the Concept of Fair

Hello? How is it that fifty-fifty is no longer the standard of fairness? Many of us thought we had egalitarian relationships only to find that, once we had kids, our marriages slipped into more traditional roles. Even those of us with very modern relationships struggle with the notion that we seem to end up doing more. A husband who is doing 30 percent of the child care or domestic chores considers himself a hero. But a wife who's left with 70 percent can feel like a slave.

Why Must We Tiptoe Around?

Sometimes we just keep doing it all, not even allowing our husbands to get involved, because we're so afraid of what will happen if we ask for help. *He's a nightmare if he's sleep-deprived; he's so grumpy if he doesn't work out.* So we put up this front that we're OK, we're fine. And really we're maxed out, but we're afraid to ask, because that could lead to a big ugly drama, which is worse than just putting the kid down for his nap yet again.

Turn Off the Light and Please Stop Grabbing Me

Why is no one feeling satisfied? For women, many of us feel pressured to be the people we were before we had kids. So if our sex drive is lagging, if we don't feel we've got the same energy or desire, we feel we've failed. Conversely, if we're feeling frisky and our husbands aren't, we feel insecure and rejected. What? We're not as desirable as we were before? Complicating matters, everyone's just trying to gauge what's normal. We all hear whispers about the couple who has crazy sex every night— what's wrong with us? Why aren't we? The final straw is the media frenzy around hot, sexy celebrity moms getting their bodies back in shape in two weeks. We don't really enjoy finding copies of *Men's Health* or *GQ* and/or other magazines with übermodels overflowing their push-up bras on the nightstand or in his gym bag.

What's So Hard about Saying Thanks?

How hard is it to say, "Thank you for making dinner" or "Thank you for taking such good care of the kids"? At the same time, we're guilty of not thanking our husbands more for all that they do. We heard this from everybody. Says one mom, "I would love to hear, 'Thanks for everything you do every day' or 'Thanks for taking care of that.' There's never enough thanks for the little things we do every day. I say, 'You know, it would be nice if you said thanks for picking up your stuff,' and he'll say, 'I didn't realize it got done' or 'I didn't realize I needed to say something.' Well, now you know."

we've set for them. They come home to a domestic environment in which we are boss. And to make matters worse, we're a mess.

We're not just talking physically, from all the spit-up and smushed macaroni and cheese. Often we're transferring all the angst we feel about our work lives, or lack of work lives, into our roles as director of parenting and executive of the house. Our men don't necessarily share our vision (for example, that the home must be perfect at all times, even with infants and toddlers; that kids must be fast-tracked, academically and otherwise), nor should they. That would be dysfunctional. But ignoring our vision may incur our wrath. As one dad proclaimed, "I come home, and it's like I'm entering into my other job where I'm the subordinate on probation, hoping to just get by. I don't feel very valued. I try to help, but I'm not doing it the way that she does, so I feel like I'm doing it wrong."

DIRTY LITTLE SECRET

I don't know how to ask for help. I just know how to scream at my husband.

Just as we compare ourselves to other mothers, we also compare our husbands to other husbands. And not the lousy ones. We compare them to the ones who are doing all the things we wish our husbands did, and this just exacerbates the situation. For example, we think, "My best friend's husband took his two toddlers to Disneyland by himself, packed for them, the whole thing. I wish my husband would or could do that." This kind of thinking builds up quiet anger, and our husbands bear the wrath. As one dad said, "She doesn't directly say it, but I hear the little comments she makes about this dad making breakfast every Saturday morning or that dad packing up the kids and taking them to the beach for the day. You know what? I'm not that dad."

MAYBE OUR HUSBANDS ARE ON TO SOMETHING

Just as we've done to ourselves as moms, we've raised the bar for being a "good dad" unreasonably high. We know this is nuts and that we really do need to get a handle on ourselves, but we do have some immutable expectations and a long roster of pet peeves. For instance, we don't get it when they're reading the paper while the kids play at their feet. We don't understand why the same man who can juggle multiple accounts at work asks us how to shampoo the kids' hair. We realize different people have different ways of connecting with children, but is ESPN really one of the best? And really, do men turn deaf when they're sleeping? How can they not hear that baby screaming in the middle of the night?

A person could reasonably argue that the above "infractions"—newspaper, TV, sleep—are our spouses' attempts to limit the amount of time and energy they feel they must give. This—setting reasonable limits—would be a logical thing to do. If we had any sense, we would do it ourselves.

From the Frontlines
She said:

My husband walks in the door and immediately says, "OK! Everyone needs to calm down! Everyone needs to lower their voices!" Are you kidding me?

SAMANTHA / 3 CHILDREN, PHILADELPHIA, PA

I know that I don't do a good-enough job of recognizing him for everything he does. In a marriage with kids, a lot of times I just want credit for the fact that I was up all night, I'm doing a conference call at 8 A.M., I'm writing stupid thank-you cards, and I'm organizing the birthday party on Saturday. Well, I think that men are the same way. I definitely don't give him enough credit, and I should. For Steve, in his mind, he's doing something for the family, for the house. Whether it's going to Costco or building radiator covers in the garage, he's probably feeling like he's not getting credit for it. I don't want him to think that this is extra credit. I want him to think it's part of his job.

SHERRY / 2 CHILDREN, ATLANTIC HIGHLANDS, NJ

My husband said, "Honey, why don't you go take a shower? You deserve it." And I said, "That's like saying, 'Honey, go take a crap. You deserve it.'" A shower is a necessity, not a luxury.

KRISTY / 4 CHILDREN, SAN ANSELMO, CA

My husband's mantra is "Happy Wife, Happy Life." He can clue in to what makes me happy and supports that.

DENISE / 3 CHILDREN, SAN DIEGO, CA

It's been my experience that the role of the mother is so extremely different. I manage and oversee their entire lives, their rituals, the things that need to be done. I need to say to him, "Oh, can you give them a bath?" In our scenario, he's the fun guy; he'll spend all day with our son and come home and have forgotten to feed him lunch!

KELLY / 2 CHILDREN, TEMPE, AZ

He said:

I feel pressure to say "thank you" to her for keeping up the house, but how come I don't ever get a thank you for working so hard to make money?

JACK / 2 CHILDREN, FARMINGTON HILLS, MI

She thinks I should know exactly what to do without being asked. Like yesterday, getting ready to go to LEGOland, I thought I was doing a good job, but I guess I wasn't. I said, "Well, you know what, we can buy snacks when we get there if I didn't pack them!" And that didn't help. I manage to get by when she's not around. I know she thinks, "I know you're smart enough to do complex surgery—so what the hell happened with the snack pack?"

PAT / 3 CHILDREN, MADISON, NJ

I just want that woman back—that woman who used to jump my bones. I just want her to want me.

EVAN / 3 CHILDREN, SAN DIEGO, CA

I think my wife understands, for the most part, what I'm going through. I can't ever be in her shoes. She can't ever truly be in mine. You can try to empathize. As long as she appreciates what I'm going through and I appreciate her, we're good.

MARK / 2 CHILDREN, DETROIT, MI

When I walk in the door from work, my wife jumps at me with a million questions and things we need to talk about. I finally was able to ask her to wait until the kids go to bed and then spend ten minutes talking about what needs to get done. That has made our nighttime routine so much happier.

TOM / 2 CHILDREN, KAUAI, HI

Sometimes my stress level gets way out of hand, and it affects everything for me. If I'm sucked into work and not going to the gym, I feel bad about myself and how I look. And that affects my desire to have sex. It's not my wife's fault, but I know somewhere deep down she feels that something's wrong with her.

NOAH / 2 CHILDREN, BOSTON, MA

So maybe, just maybe, we should try to learn a thing or two from our children's fathers instead of being antagonistic. What would happen if we turned on a DVD so we could finish a book? What if we skipped the nightly baths and went out for ice cream? What if we pretended we couldn't hear the baby in the middle of the night?

THEY WANT A MANUAL

When confronted with the overwhelming task of being a good family man, many men told us the same thing: They want a manual. They get it—they know women and men are equals. They know they're not supposed to behave like their own fathers. They just don't know what all this translates into in terms of action, and we heard this a lot from the fathers we interviewed. Men don't want to be bossed around, but they do want to know, precisely, what is expected of and needed from them. As one father put it, "That's the universal law. Man's position in life is he can never figure out what the hell he's supposed to be doing. Just give us a rule book. We can't read minds."

From our perspective, however, this is somewhat inconvenient because many mothers find it difficult to ask for help, let alone produce comprehensive instructions. And we do accept that everybody's lives would be better if we could just say, without an edge, "Hey, honey, can you grab the apples, juice, and backpack while I brush my teeth?" But let's get real:

How hard is it for a guy to read the directions on the back of the canister of baby formula? Must we produce a printed document before men realize that the dirty dishes won't load themselves into the dishwasher?

I'm so stretched in every area of my life. In order to buy the house we want, I have to be at the top of my career. I'm expected to be a hands-on dad, be at every baseball game for my son, and volunteer for my daughter's school. From my wife's perspective, I'm still not around enough.

Bill / 2 children, Chicago, IL

Adding to the marital strife, many men define *helping* on their own terms. They see driving to Home Depot for gutters as help when really we just want two extra hands to get the kids out the door. But not telling our spouses what we need and expecting them to be clairvoyant can lead to mistaken assumptions and resentment. "My wife has this anger that's just lurking there beneath the surface, and any little thing that I don't do right, or don't do at all, will trigger it," one father told us. "And the hardest part for me is that half the time, I don't even know what I'm supposed to be doing in the first place."

Don't assume that we're trying to annoy you or make your life harder. It's just that we don't always get what you're going through.

Roger / 4 children, Pittsburgh, PA

DIRTY LITTLE SECRET

I would give up my husband for a housekeeper.

5 easy steps

1. Talk about your expectations. Just understanding each other's expectations will help you manage them and, if need be, renegotiate them. Talk on a daily or weekly basis to set up what you expect of each other.

2. Let him do it his way. It's probably pretty tough dealing with our expectations, insane or otherwise. Try letting go of the idea that your husband should do everything the same way you do.

3. Realize that men talk about what they're feeling even less than we do (and we've learned that moms really aren't talking as much as they'd like). Like you, he's probably feeling a lot of pressure. Like you, he may be feeling "alone" in the family, too.

4. Let him help you. And tell him how to do it. You don't actually need to write a manual, but if you tell him what you need, you've got a lot better chance of getting it. And if you're doing everything yourself, you're enabling him not to do anything. So don't just criticize him for not helping—let him help you.

5. Cut yourself some slack if you're in a tough phase. Husbands evolve over time. Wives evolve over time. Children grow up. You will find your rhythm again. A lot has changed quickly. You'll find a new groove.

CHAPTER 7

WHEN YOU SAY *MOM*, IT LEAVES A LOT UNSAID ABOUT YOU

· · ·

(Honor Your Whole Self)

quiz no. 7

**YOU KNOW YOU'VE LOST YOURSELF
COMPLETELY WHEN . . .**

CHECK ALL THAT APPLY.

- [ ] You introduce yourself at an important business meeting as "Andrea's mom."

- [ ] You can't remember the last time you showered without two (or more) eyes on you.

- [ ] It's normal to leave the house with Barbie stickers plastered to your thigh.

- [ ] You think watching the Oscars on TV is a real night out.

- [ ] You reflexively refer to the bathroom as "the potty."

- [ ] You get competitive about winning Chutes and Ladders.

- [ ] You ask your children questions like "Do these jeans make my butt look big?"

- [ ] You find yourself rescuing a tiny LEGO man from a poopy toilet.

- [ ] You drink from a sippy cup in public.

- [ ] You catch yourself humming a Raffi song under your breath.

AMONG THE MANY STRANGE THINGS THAT HAVE HAPPENED since we each popped out a kid or two, or three, is that our names have changed. We are no longer primarily known as Amy or Trish. We are now known as Mom, and Mom is not fully considered a person, with the same needs and rights as everybody else in the family. Yes, Mom is loved, maybe even adored. But Mom—part servant, part superhero—is basically a cartoon. She's supposed to be tireless, available around the clock, and absolutely stable. She's also supposed to be sort of like the goddess Durga, with ten arms, tending to all children in need of care while at the same time cooking, dialing the phone, typing at the keyboard, and keeping the house relatively clean.

The idea of Mom as a two-dimensional figure is not something inflicted upon us by our husbands and our kids. We do it to ourselves. In fact, the only people who seem to realize that Mom is a person—a fragile, important person—are those folks who make the safety videos for airlines. We typically don't give these good people the respect they deserve, but it's not too late to take a lesson from them. Mom needs to put on her oxygen mask first. Or to put it more broadly: Mom needs to take care of herself to take care of her family.

Taking care of Mom can feel strange and counterintuitive, because Mom came into being for other people, these little people that we love. But for everybody's health and sanity, Mom needs to stop thinking of herself as a needless, tireless dispenser of food and care. Yes, of course, Mom is a caretaker, and she shouldn't keep a balance sheet about who's giving more to whom. But Mom needs to reconceive of herself as a human being. She needs to tend to her well-being—mental, emotional, and physical. She should treat herself like a member of the family, just like her spouse and kids.

If I am true to myself, I can be a good mom.

Shannon / 2 children, San Francisco, CA

Most of the women we spoke with couldn't pinpoint a moment in time when they were officially demoted to not-quite-human status, but many could name a moment when they realized it'd happened. There they were, say, checking e-mail, and up popped a note from a friend they really care about but hadn't even thought about in six months. Or they noticed their eyes flickering like a starved animal's when they heard someone talking about seeing a movie. Personally, we had to face the fact that the people formerly known as Trish and Amy had been subsumed by Mom when we realized that neither of us had read anything more substantial than *Us* magazine in six (OK, thirteen) months. We found this rather alarming, as we used to love to read, but noticing it wasn't enough to fix the problem. We found it hard to get back in touch with ourselves. Part of the difficulty was trying to figure out who we were trying to get back in touch with—so much had changed since we really knew who we were. But we made a pact to remind each other that we're not robots and that we need to take care of our whole selves—all the messy, conflicting, inconvenient parts that make us people worth loving.

DIRTY LITTLE SECRET

Sometimes I secretly let the milk run out so that I have to make a late-night grocery run—all by myself. I drive slowly, put the windows down, and enjoy a tiny piece of solitude.

Just because a woman has created a new life doesn't mean she should lose herself. She should be proud, maybe even transformed and filled with love. But she should still be an independent person. Somehow, for most of us, this idea got put away forever with our prepregnancy jeans.

When we asked moms how they were doing, we often heard things like, "Oh, my kids are great; everything is great!" So we pressed. "No, no—how are *you* doing?" After this, we typically heard a rather long pause. Moms often use their kids' happiness as a proxy for how they're feeling themselves. Of course, if a woman's kids are unwell, she's probably not great herself. But just because her kids are feeling fine doesn't mean she is, too.

Just saying you're a mom says you like changing diapers and there's nothing interesting about you. *Mom* leaves a lot out about who I am. I am a great athlete.

Karyn / 2 children, Kentfield, CA

When we asked moms to define themselves, we first heard a lot of roles—mother, wife, friend, caregiver. So we pressed again, and this time, after the pause, there was often a moment of realization and confusion, because frequently who a woman is on the inside, to herself, is fairly different from the roles she plays. As Dawn put it, "I think it's interesting that I can't define myself easily, as a mother, wife, by my career. It's true that a lot of what I do best I do in all those roles. But I still feel like there are a lot of things I'm putting off figuring out about who I am and who I want to be because I'm putting my family and my job before me as an individual."

Some women pour their whole selves into being moms, and the phenomenon of the mother so good and so devoted she's actually disserving her children is one that's well known to family psychologists. "So many moms will not give themselves permission to take care of themselves. And I get really strong with my terminology. I say that is very harmful to your children," says psychologist Shoshana Bennett, coauthor of *Beyond the Blues: A Guide to Understanding and Treating Prenatal and Postpartum Depression.* "Often women need to hear how much taking care of themselves will benefit the kids. They think it's selfish to take care of themselves. Sometimes moms who are depressed are only willing to put themselves on the calendar if it's for the kids. So, I'll say, 'Yes, do it for the kids. Otherwise they'll have a burned-out, wiped-out mother, and that's not the best thing for the child.'"

Motherhood is still harder than I would have ever imagined. My identity is all out of whack. I really enjoyed my job before, and now I feel guilty if I sit and watch *Oprah* for ten seconds.

Carla / 2 children, Fort Worth, TX

Many moms we talked to had a hard time detangling the idea of selfishness from the idea of taking care of themselves. They told us they hadn't been to the gym in a year because their children needed them. They told us they'd just feel too guilty and pampered if they hired a sitter even once a month so they could spend some adult-only time with friends. Hello?! These things should not feel selfish. They're critical to staying sane in a demanding adult life.

I had a moment after I quit working [after] my second child. I had a fainting spell, and I was lying in the stretcher, and I could hear the hospital staff interviewing my husband about me, and he said I was a housewife. And I yelled, "What did you call me? Don't ever call me that!" And he said, "Well, that's what you are!"

MONICA / 2 CHILDREN, LOS ANGELES, CA

If you have time to shave one leg, it's a miracle. If you have time to shave two, you feel guilty.

SHELLY / 3 CHILDREN, HOUSTON, TX

In reclaiming yourself, it's important to remember who you are in the first place: the woman who loves to read books, or hike, or blast Elton John really loud. Often we think of defining ourselves in terms of core values and priorities, and that's important. But one mother we spoke to suggested a simpler method. She tried to remember who she was by getting back in touch with what she called her "likable self." You know that woman you like hanging out with, alone in a café, giggling at a private joke? That's who we're talking about. *She's* who you're trying to reclaim.

Expectations have a way of parting mothers from their likable selves, so it's important to figure out which parts of you developed directly from others' expectations and which parts are central to your being—the parts you want to hang on to, the parts that are pristine and real. You'll still have to take into account other people's desires and needs. It's just that motherhood often throws us into a cyclone of activity in which we believe we have no time to do anything personal except (maybe) pee. This experience was really brought home for us by one mom named Marcy: "My son was five weeks old, and I dove back into consulting, on autopilot, juggling the newborn stuff, taking care of the house and dog. All of a sudden, out of nowhere, I had a total breakdown and wondered why. Then I woke up one day and realized that I never even asked myself, 'Is this what I want? Is this the best thing for me? Is this fulfilling me? Do I even like myself?'"

Finding ourselves in lives that feel strange is partly the fault of having children, but not entirely. Too many mothers we spoke with described themselves as being on autopilot or feeling that their real selves were put away in a box. They told us about driving the cars best suited to their

DIRTY LITTLE SECRET

I want my own apartment because I don't like people touching my stuff. And I would prefer if my husband didn't visit.

children, living in houses furnished to their children's taste, and spending their days in ways that made their children marginally happy but left them feeling like they were quietly losing it. Even moms of slightly older children told us the same thing—their kids were running their lives, and they still weren't giving themselves permission to sit down and read a book or take a nap. One mother even told us about finding herself one day, several years into motherhood, wearing an ugly purple sweater her daughter's babysitter had given her for Christmas, because her daughter liked purple. "I just kind of looked down at this too-big cabled lavender thing and lost it. I should be able to still dress for myself, right?"

I DON'T TELL EVERYONE THAT I PUT MYSELF FIRST— THEY'D BE HORRIFIED

The great thing about deciding you're ready to be a person again is that you already are one. You just need to give yourself permission to start acting the part. That's right, *you* need to give yourself permission to be an important person. *You* need to honor yourself. No sense in waiting for your husband or your mother or your kids to tell you it's time to take care of yourself.

Taking off the Mom mantle and tending to your whole person is harder than it sounds because, as Bennett says, "There's a lot of self-doubt in general, especially with new moms. Am I doing it right? Is that mom so much better than me? Can I afford to give myself a break?" What Bennett tells her clients is to get the opinions out of their heads. "You can practice this. Get the voices out—your mom, your friends—and ask what is it that you truly want. When a woman gives herself permission to do that, really do that, there's such a look of amazement, and then relief."

Complicating the process of reclaiming one's self is the fact that we've changed so much since we had kids. Thus, becoming a person again may involve grieving for the woman you were before you had kids and embracing the human being you are now. So, although it's important to be attuned to what made us feel whole in our past lives—jogging, meditating, practicing spirituality, working, and so on—we also need to acknowledge our new realities. After having children, we may need quiet more than we need a night out. We may need an intellectual outlet. We may need to sit on a park bench and do nothing at all.

I did a lot of work, before I had kids, trying to figure out what was right for me in the work world, or what I was truly passionate about. There were tangible ways I knew I could reclaim who I really am. I've taken time away from my job, but I'm starting to write again. When I get a little of everything is a good day—a little mommy time, a little exercise, a little writing.

Annie / 2 children, Greenbrae, CA

The key is to define your needs and then commit to them. Yes, *commit to your own needs,* and you must start by tuning out others' perceptions of what's valuable, necessary, and a worthy use of time in your life. Part of what you're trying to teach your children is how to be a whole, well-rounded human being, and doing so requires self-knowledge, self-care, and self-respect. As an adult, it's your job to figure out how to nurture yourself. And once you figure *that* out, you need to honor it.

Every two months or so, I go to see a therapist. Here is somebody getting paid, with no agenda. She'll sit and listen and sympathize and give me a chance to vent and take stock. I always walk away feeling so much better. The things I complain about sound so petty when I say them out loud. It's my reality perspective check.

RACHEL / 3 CHILDREN, WELLESLEY, MA

I said, "Mom, I'm losing it; I don't know who I am," and she said, "No matter what happens, you always come back to yourself. You will never lose yourself." And she was right; I always come back to me.

KIM / 3 CHILDREN, MADISON, NJ

I don't tell everyone that I put myself first—they'd be horrified by that. Why do so many other moms not understand that? For me, everything comes back to the core self. If I'm not taking care of myself first, I can't be a good wife, a good mom. I rank myself first, then my relationship; the kid thing is third because it's the most natural thing to put my attention to.

SHANNON / 2 CHILDREN, SAN FRANCISCO, CA

10 simple ways

1. Ask yourself, "Who am I *today*?" Don't put pressure on yourself to reclaim who you were before you had kids. Start to figure out who you are now.

2. Remember who you are *not*. "I am not my mother; I am not my sister; I am not my best friend."

3. Put up a family calendar and block out time for yourself, just like you'd schedule a doctor's appointment. Let everyone know that this time is inflexible and important.

4. Redefine what success means. If you're truly doing your best at that moment, even if it might be below your usual standards, then you've succeeded.

5. Learn to feel compassion for yourself. Motherhood is not easy—applaud yourself for your accomplishments, and have empathy for yourself when you're having a hard time. Compassion for yourself will breed compassion for others.

6. Get back in touch with your goals in life, and spend time working on them, even if you can only take baby steps.

to Honor Your Whole Self

7. Appreciate the best parts of yourself. Even when you're feeling remorse over screaming at your kid, know that you're a good person at your core. What do your closest friends say they love about you? What do they lean on you for?

8. When the going gets tough, give yourself a time-out. We've heard from many moms that they do this when they're about to snap. No matter what, they make sure the kids are safe for a few minutes, and they go in another room, shut the door, and just breathe, cry, scream, kick—whatever they need to do.

9. Trust yourself. Know that you won't let yourself down. Give up the urge to think you need fourteen books on motherhood or your child's acceptance to three preschools before you'll know what you're doing.

10. Focus on what brings you pure joy.

CHAPTER 8

YOU KNOW WHAT? IT AIN'T GONNA HAPPEN

. . .

(Just Say No)

quiz no. 8

HAVE YOU EVER SAID YES TO ANY OF THE FOLLOWING (WHEN YOU REALLY WANTED TO SAY NO)?

- [ ] Throwing a baby shower for a friend you don't even like that much.

- [ ] Hosting a playdate with your son's buddy . . . and his two sisters.

- [ ] Volunteering to head up the set design for your daughter's school play while you've got a newborn strapped to your chest.

- [ ] Pet-sitting your neighbor's mouthy, barking puppy.

- [ ] Attending a business dinner with your husband's boring colleagues.

- [ ] Hosting your book club every month because the members like your lasagna.

- [ ] Flying across the country to stay with your in-laws for two weeks.

- [ ] Buying ridiculously overpriced superhero and princess costumes.

- [ ] Having sex.

SAYING NO IS ONE OF THOSE THINGS THAT IS BOTH VERY SIMPLE and very complex. We've all said it a million times. We've said no out of love, out of anger, out of frustration, exhaustion, peace, and rage. *N-O.* No way. Can't do it. We'll pass. Not for us. Please accept our regrets. Sorry. Back off. Ain't gonna happen.

Saying no is a talent every mother needs to develop in her own life. Or redevelop—we were all adept at saying no as toddlers, and geniuses at it (at least to our parents) during our adolescent years. But mothers find saying no especially difficult. And it's worth taking the time to understand why that is so we can make more conscious decisions about when we should really say yes.

Part of the difficulty of saying no stems from the you-can-do-it-all mentality. If we think we can or should be able to work, raise kids, nurture relationships, and participate in our communities, how can we possibly decline a neighbor's fortieth-birthday-party invitation or say we're too busy to read during story time in a child's class? Maybe we could say no if we knew we had planned a crucial meeting or had scheduled a trip out of town. But what if the reason we're declining is that we plan to be lounging on the couch watching a DVD with our husband? Or sitting on a park bench with our kid?

The typical mom is expected to do a lot of stuff that nobody in her right mind would choose to do. As a result, moms get out of practice at drawing boundaries and making logical decisions about what's right for them. The word *no* can come to symbolize being a bad mother, bad daughter, bad wife, or bad friend. So we avoid saying no because we don't want to take on those labels. Moreover, we don't say no when we should because we don't want to create conflict, disappoint, or be judged. But never saying no has very real costs. Topping the list, being a yes-woman breeds bitterness and anger because we inevitably find ourselves in situations we don't want to be in. Sure, saying no means letting some people down. But remember that we will also let people down—ourselves and our families—if we always say yes.

When I'm with the kids, I'm in the moment with them, and that's because I love the balance that I have. On the days when I'm working, I set aside time to get things done. When I'm with my kids, it's set in my mind that it's their time. I do *no* professional work at home. I don't talk on the phone during my time with them.

Jennifer / 2 children, Chicago, IL

Professionals such as family therapist Shelly Breger have known this was a problem for a long time:

> *What I've been hearing is that there are many educated women who have held very important jobs who have either cut back on workloads or given up their jobs, and they're having a very hard time saying no. This is my take on it. They think: Now my job is "I'm going to be the best mother I can possibly be. I am going to do everything in my*

DIRTY LITTLE SECRET

I tell lies. Soccer's been canceled; we can't go. Or the pool's not open; we can't go.

*power to make it perfect." So when the school asks her to
be the room mother and run an auction, she says yes. And if
the church or synagogue asks her to teach a Sunday school
class, she says yes. And if her child needs oranges and water
for soccer, she says yes. And if she can drive because the
class is going to the petting zoo, she says yes.*

The reason for saying yes so often, according to Breger, is that when
many mothers say no, they're not living up to their vision of being *the
good mother*—the mother who is all-encompassing and can take care of
her home and her children and still manage all the outside activities she's
asked to do. And this causes problems:

*All the energy goes out—to the children, the community,
service, husbands who travel—and nothing goes in to the
relationship. And a lot of marriages fail early. They used to
fail when kids went off to college. Now they fail when the
kids are little. The "no" piece is such an important piece. I've
had so many moms walk in and say, "OK, I need to practice saying no. Help me practice." I say to them, "OK, what
are you being asked to do? And what do you really want to
do?" Mothers need to ask themselves these questions.*

YOU CAN'T BE EVERYBODY'S FULL-TIME MOM

Think of it this way: By saying no, you're actually saying yes to something
else, something that you'd rather do or need to do more, something that
will make your life how you want it to be. For almost all of us, the desire
to say no does not come out of malice. We don't say no because we want
to disappoint. We want to say no because opting out of whatever it is will
make life better for us and our families.

No means getting to sleep on time. *No* means spending the day
together as a family. *No* means a calmer, less-hectic evening leading to
calmer, less-harried kids.

It's hard for me to say no, but I do find that for my daughter, if she's got too many things going on, she's a bloody mess for days! So I work hard at not overprogramming my kids. I didn't have that growing up. I remember being bored, but I read a ton; I created my own things. People rattle off all the things they have their kids doing. I let my kids pick one thing they like, and that's it.

KAREN / 3 CHILDREN, PITTSBURGH, PA

I have finally learned that there's not enough time in the day for everything. So I ask myself, What am I getting out of that friend? And I just have to let them go sometimes.

BRIDGETT / 2 CHILDREN, HOUSTON, TX

Setting some clear rules to live by will help you figure out when to say no and when to say yes. What does your family need to function happily? You should be saying yes to things that move you toward honoring those rules and no to things that cause you to break them.

If a mother is feeling like she should say yes to something but her gut is screaming *No! No! No!* she should put the obligation in question to the happy-family test. Will the obligation—volunteering at church, going out to dinner with cousins—move her toward the goal of a happy (and functioning) family? Yes? No? There's the answer. As a mother named Jennifer told us, "I was listening to a mom the other day who was bragging about having to go to four dance recitals, and I thought, 'Well, good for you, but we're going home to eat dinner and do homework.'"

At times the word *no* is not what anybody's expecting to hear. One mother told us that she recently turned back—yes, drove partway and then turned back—from going out to dinner to celebrate her grandmother's ninety-eighth birthday because it would have left her infant and toddler daughters a wreck before they caught a plane the following day. This is not a decision everybody would make, but she knew her boundaries for her family. The happy-family test might make some people in your life feel like low priorities, and—you know what?—so be it. Most of the time even Grandma will understand.

Our lives as contemporary mothers are seriously overcommitted. We've got too many things to do. Our obligations need pruning, and saying no is the shears. Mothers we've spoken to who are reining in the family chaos have found themselves saying no to taking a niece to ballet class, no to hosting an extensive birthday party, and no to joining the company picnic. Many mothers say they need to learn to say no to their own mothers in order to put their new families first. For instance, Krista told us how her husband always felt like he was last in line and waiting for her to throw him a bone. "He said, 'Well, you're so anxious to make your parents happy that you never made that transition. Now *this* is your core. We are your core.'"

When I was a full-time mom, I became a full-time mom for everybody. I helped my brother look for a house. I helped my grandma with her doctors. Everyone thought of me as the person who could take care of it.

Kiersten / 2 children, Los Angeles, CA

Granted, if a mother repeatedly says no to the same person, that person may start to get the impression that she is not at the top of the list, and that's OK, too. The goal should be a life that reflects your family's priorities and values. A woman can't be a very effective mother to a particular child if she's trying to take care of the whole world.

WAFFLING IS TORTURE

Who you're saying no to can affect your resolve, especially if they're your own kids. One mother we spoke with, Stella, told us she had this down pat. "Saying no to the kids is easy. Saying no to other parents is a little trickier. You're making a judgment call about their decisions."

For many mothers, however, saying no to their children is especially tricky; it's inextricably bound up in the desire to make the kids feel loved (and to feel loved back). We don't want to be the bad guys. And sometimes, if we were absent all afternoon (or tense all afternoon!), we might say yes to the playdate or the extra cookie just because we feel guilty.

DIRTY LITTLE SECRET

I told my daughter I have invisible eyes in the back of my head and I can see everything she's doing. She believed me and asked if she was going to have them also when she's a grown-up. I said yes.

Yet indiscriminately saying yes to our children can be counter-productive. It might stave off a tantrum or meet a short-term need, but parents must set boundaries and rules for their households. This builds an environment that's solid, safe, warm, and secure, both physically and emotionally. As therapist Breger says, "You're the person who sets the limits, the moral code, the ethical boundaries, who teaches manners. And you have to say no. 'No, you can't have a sleepover. You'll sleep at Josh's tomorrow. No, you can't go on this ski trip. We can't afford it.' We've lost our compass here! It's our job to help them become self-sufficient." And that means teaching them how to set limits and make good decisions for themselves.

A key tactic that has helped a lot of mothers is to say no with conviction, and stick to it. Make it a confident no, not a wimpy no. In three days, or two minutes, don't change your mind. Especially with children, it's important not to back down. Many of us have experienced the "waffling phenomenon." When you begin to waffle, you lose all control and credibility. Your children will see your vulnerability, and they'll launch an initiative to break your resolve, and the decision will ultimately be much harder on you all. Says Allison from Houston, "My kids can see right through me. When I initially said no to her swimming playdate, she was fine, but the minute I started to waffle, it was torture. She could see that I was questioning my own no—why shouldn't she go swimming? I might be robbing her of a really fun time. All her friends are going; why can't she? When I finally put my foot down, she broke down in tears."

The idea of firmness leads us to an important point: Don't think saying "maybe" will buy you anything, sister. All maybe does is put off the inevitable and string somebody along. Once you've made your decision, better to just get it over with, like a shot: a little pinch and it's done. One mom, Tina, regularly finds herself on the fence and hates it. "Why do I do that to myself?" she asks. "I waver and say maybe when deep down I really just don't want to do it. Then I get roped into all these things I don't want to do and end up mad at that person when it's not even her fault. It's my fault for not just saying no."

It's taken me a long time to shut out the noise. Now I do say things like, "Well, I'm really happy that it works for your family, but we're just not there yet." Or "We're not doing it that way." I don't want to have to revisit things. "Why isn't your kid going to that party?" I just want to say right away, "She's not going because we're not comfortable with it," and leave it at that.

Rachel / 2 children, New York, NY

And saying no, firmly, to our own parents can be the hardest of all. We know exactly what they expect of us, and rejecting that bluntly can be really tough. But, moms, trust us on this: Once you learn to say no to your own mother, some of the pressure will lift and you will feel great. For instance, just last year, Margaret was just too crazed to get a Christmas card together, and her mom would not let up. She kept saying, "Well, if you're too busy right now, maybe you could put a Valentine's Day card together with a picture of the kids. Or maybe Easter? *Everyone* expects a card from you, *everyone* wants to see how the children have grown." Margaret finally had to say, "You know what, Mom? It ain't gonna happen. Not this year, not for any holiday." And that was incredibly liberating, to just say it straight—no. End of discussion.

DIRTY LITTLE SECRET

I tell my daughter, "You are only two years old. It says right here on the package you can only have two cookies."

I hadn't found the right rhythm with my kids until about a year ago. I was just trying to make everyone happy, and I didn't have my priorities straight. Then Mike said, "Let's prioritize the things that matter, and say no to the things that aren't critical." We made a rule that we would never make plans on a Sunday. That conversation helped me see I was making a choice to put my family first.

KRISTA / 2 CHILDREN, YARDLEY, PA

6 simple steps

1. When you say no, let it go. Don't harbor anything. Let go of the guilt associated with saying no.

2. When you say no, back it up with why, and make the why real, not an excuse. If you're just feeling a bit overstretched and need some downtime, it's okay to say so. So many times we say yes to something because we just don't have another event at that time.

3. Recognize situations where you want to say no and end up saying yes. To build your confidence in saying no, remember that you're refusing the request, not the person.

4. Remember that you can't be everything to everybody. Saying yes to everything means being overbooked, overstressed, and anxious.

5. Ask yourself if the request is a real need and, if it is, whether the person needs you in particular. Sometimes, even when a request isn't a real need, we interpret it as such in our heads. Or we flatter ourselves by thinking we're indispensable, when in reality we're not.

6. Don't confuse saying yes with being a nice person. We think we're being gracious by saying yes to everything, but committing to things we can't deliver on only leads to bitterness and disappointment.

CHAPTER 9

OH MY GOD, I DON'T WANT TO COLOR RIGHT NOW

● ● ●

(Live in the Moment)

quiz no. 9

WHEN WAS THE LAST TIME YOU . . .

CHECK ALL THAT APPLY.

☐ Enjoyed a kid's birthday without worrying about taking pictures?

☐ Played hooky to go to the movies?

☐ Had a dance party in the living room?

☐ Declared a pajama day?

☐ Laughed till you cried?

☐ Stopped for a lunch date with your child on the way home from school?

☐ Let your kids bury you in the sand?

☐ Turned off your cell phone?

☐ Started a snowball or water fight?

☐ Made breakfast for dinner?

WE'VE ALL MANAGED TO LIVE IN THE MOMENT AT SOME POINT.
We've lingered on the steps in front of the preschool and talked to our three-year-old about the clouds. Or we've lain in the grass and looked at the flowers. Or we've sat on the floor with the mini kingdom set and played knight and princess like we had all the time in the world. Maybe we were on vacation, or we'd just wrapped up a major project. Whatever it was, that constantly revving engine inside us finally slowed down. The pressure subsided, the to-do list disappeared, and our children, who are always the most important things in our lives—in thought, if not always in action—actually came front and center.

We've also all failed to do this, a lot. We've pushed the kids out the door to school. We've tried to make work calls in the bathroom while the baby's in the bath. We've spent entire Saturdays preoccupied with reorganizing our garages and told our kids, no, we can't play dress-up right now. And chances are, those days turned out to be a lot less fun. What's worse, those moments probably felt pretty normal—we all do these things all the time. Not just that, we all *need* to do these things all the time. We need to multitask. If we just focused on each single moment, one at a time, we'd need at least a seventy-two-hour day.

But consider what happens when we actually put other concerns at bay—for ten minutes, for half an hour, for an afternoon—and just focus on our kids. Yes, the dirty dishes stay in the sink, or the haircut appointment does not get made, but the payoff is immense. Those minutes spent playing fort under the dining room table are not only the best part of our children's days, but they're the best part of our days, too. One mother, Tori, told us a story that seems near biblical in its concision. She was busy cleaning up her house, and her six-year-old daughter asked, "Mom, can you sew this button on my pants?" Tori's instinct was to say no. But she dropped what she was doing, sat down, and sewed the button on. Her daughter looked up at her and said, "Mom, you're my hero." As Tori recounted, "It was amazing how stopping to put on a button made such a huge difference to her."

MOM'S A LITTLE NUTS. SORRY, BUDDY.

Why don't we live in the moment more often? Our insane expectations leave us running off in all directions almost all the time. Really, how can we possibly stare lovingly into our six-month-old baby's eyes, rolling around on the floor, when eight loads of laundry need washing, the dog is barking, the phone is ringing, and our older son's playdate is knocking on the door?

Most of the time we're not even aware that we're not in the moment. Most of the time we're just coasting on cruise control, with our practical side doing the steering. Baths. Homework. Bed. Get up. Breakfast. Get dressed. Out the door. Leave younger kid at day care. Drop older kid

DIRTY LITTLE SECRET

My life is so crazy and I practically live in my car. I'm mortified to admit this, but there are some days I don't even have time to pee . . . so I wear Depends!

at preschool. Work. Retrieve kids and engage them in activity. Clean the house. Buy birthday present. Grocery shop. Make dinner. Then do it again.

Eventually, though, many of us get exhausted, and we realize there's got to be another way. One mother, Allison, had a dramatic wake-up call after years spent juggling two kids and a demanding job: she started having chest pains. Turned out she had a stress-related inflammatory disease. But getting off the perpetual-motion machine and living in the moment was not so easy. "My transition from full-time work to stay-at-home mom was filled with tragic, hysterical stories," she told us. "One day I left my son in Staples because I literally forgot about him, and I started to drive off, and he was standing there in front of the store like, 'What are you, nuts?' And I was like, 'Yeah, well, Mom is a little nuts, Dan. Sorry, buddy.'"

Maybe you haven't actually left your kid at the mall, but her point is one we can all relate to. "I was just on a treadmill, and I couldn't or wouldn't get off," Allison goes on. "My big thing now is that it's *impossible* to juggle it all. Multitasking is a crock."

The question is how to slow down in our daily lives when there is an enormous amount that needs to get done. Unless the housekeeper of our dreams suddenly swoops down from the sky, the key for many of us is to find a way to savor the dailiness. To stop rushing through all the mundane duties we do have to do, to stop thinking that when we finish, the good stuff will start. Because the truth is, the good stuff is already here. It's like the old Zen koan: Before enlightenment, chop wood, carry water. After enlightenment, chop wood, carry water. And despite our motherly workloads (which, indeed, may never end but merely change shape), we can find joy daily in the smaller moments we used to take for granted. For example, driving your child to school can be a nice time for a conversation. A bath is an excellent opportunity to check in with a child at the end of the day. We're so used to running from one thing to the next, trying to eke out some room at the end for something special, that we don't

I'm always saying to her, "OK—just a second!" So I try to sit down and do a project where she has my undivided attention. But it's hard because then the laundry just falls between the cracks, the phone is ringing constantly. I'm here a lot physically, but spending uninterrupted time with her is really hard.

BRIDGETT / 2 CHILDREN, HOUSTON, TX

When they're still sleeping with their butts in the air, the drool coming out of their mouths, it's so cute, and you get it.

GRACY / 2 CHILDREN, CHARLOTTE, NC

always take advantage of the time we do have. Our kids want our love and attention, whenever and wherever. We need to remember that these special moments can occur whenever we make them.

IF I'M THEIR ROLE MODEL, THAT'S NOT A GOOD THING

Another important thing for us all to remember is that our children are watching us for cues on how to live. You know those curses you've heard coming out of your three-year-old's mouth? Or that funny way she moves her hands that's just like you? Well, our children also look to us to figure out how to enjoy their own lives, to decide what's valuable in their days. Do you want your children to think of a rainbow as a photo op or do you want them to learn how to pause and appreciate the beauty that's before them right now?

Without getting too philosophical, in a very real sense now is all we've got. We can't change the past and we can't predict the future. Today is the only time we can control, so we might as well devote as much as we can to what we're doing in the present. As Eckhart Tolle, best-selling author of *The Power of Now,* has said, "We spend our days dwelling on past mistakes—why did I have to eat that double cheeseburger?—or fretting about the future—the high school reunion is coming up, and I just ate that double cheeseburger." Lost in all that worrying is the present, the only period we can actually experience and enjoy at any given moment. "The now is the only thing there ever is, you can't get away from it," says Tolle. "But the voice in our head keeps us either in the past or in the future, treating the present moment as if it were the enemy."

Yes, yes, we know: Children by their very nature encourage us to think about the future. And every parent does need to plan ahead. But sometimes, dwelling on the past and worrying about the future take over our thoughts—and our actions as well. Wouldn't it feel better to have a great moment now instead of thinking about one that may or may not happen in two days, two weeks, or two years? Of course, somebody does need to call the dentist and enroll the kids in kindergarten, but equally important is carving out time to play horses with a five-year-old. Because *that's* what you're going to look back on fondly, not the great worrying you did over where you sent her to camp.

At the end of the day, I don't even remember if I kissed one of them good-bye this morning. It's always so rush-rush. I feel guilty about not being a little more loving during the day, just going through the motions instead of asking how they're feeling. It makes me feel like I'm not being a very nice person. If I'm their role model, that's not a good thing.

Reyna / 2 children, New York, NY

IF I PLAY CANDY LAND ONE MORE TIME I WILL DEFINITELY BARF

But let's get real: Playing with horses is not always that compelling. Most of us would probably prefer to read the latest issue of *People* rather than slog through *Curious George* once again. So we'll say that unspeakable thing: More than occasionally, we retreat from our children's activities *not* because we can't do them, but because we don't want to. Part of the reason we don't live in the moment is that the moment before us is not really what we want. In truth, the moment before us is often not our moment at all, but our children's moment, and we resist it.

So you never want to hear Raffi again? Or you think if you play Candy Land one more time, you will definitely barf? It helps to remember that this moment, whatever it is, is fleeting. This phase will quickly pass, especially with young children. Just when you think you've got it down, everything will change.

DIRTY LITTLE SECRET

I've locked my kids in the car not once, not twice, but three times.

How Do Moms Live in the Moment?

"I try not to schedule certain days, and just go with the flow with the kids, which can sometimes mean staying in and playing with their toys if that's what they seem happy doing. I try to remember that just because I like to keep busy doesn't necessarily mean that they do!"

"We try and walk or bike to school every morning. It's a nice and slower-paced way to start the day."

"Every day we have 'hug and kiss' time—this makes me feel like, no matter what happens with the day, I have had my 'moment.'"

"We have two rituals every day: In the morning, we watch *Mister Rogers' Neighborhood,* and we like singing the end song together: 'It's such a good feeling, to know you're alive. . . .' And at the dinner table each night, we play 'good day, bad day.' It's fun, hearing a three-year-old's responses to what was good and bad about her day."

"When my husband is away I make breakfast for dinner, and that is a huge hit. Other times I'll climb in the bath with them, and they think it's hilarious."

"The best way for me to live in the moment is to stop talking and listen to my son. Leave space for his thought process to work and reveal itself. When I do that, I get the reward of seeing the world through his eyes, which is magnificent!"

"Walking together, looking at the blue sky: 'Is the sky smooth, Mama?' Bicycling together: 'I feel so free-e-e-e-e, Mama! I feel like I'm flying!' It's the greatest gift."

"I sit on the bed with my daughter and we playact with her vast collection of stuffed animals. We really *are* the characters. It's fun together time, and my daughter gets to be the director, which means she can boss me around. In the moment, this brings great joy to her life and makes me laugh."

Focusing on the idea that life is a series of (very short) phases can help breed patience and keep a mother from feeling trapped. As one mom put it, "It's hard—the day in, day out. I'm thinking, 'Oh my God, I don't want to color right now.' But if I just spend twenty minutes on an art project with her, then she [gets] her fix, and she's better off for the rest of the day."

Wrapped up in our resistance to living in our children's moments are the anger and frustration we may feel about the way our children's phases hamper ours. For instance, we heard from Piper that after she had her baby, her "whole diatribe was, 'We don't go on adventures; let's pack up the baby and go camping.'" Now, she says, "I'm much more comfortable with the smaller things. I'm happy to sit in the lawn chair and barbecue in the backyard together. I realized that time is scarce together, so we don't need to be in a hotel or packing a bag or climbing a mountain. I was grasping on to my old independence. And now I know it is OK; it's just different."

Personally, when we're feeling exasperated, we like to think in terms of "the last time"—as in, there will be a last time for everything. When will be the last time I give her a bottle, or the last time I put her to bed in her crib, or the last time I can actually cradle my son in my lap, or the last time he will let me hold his hand in public? It's amazing how quickly this puts things in perspective. One minute we're thinking we'll have to shoot ourselves if we have to dress her up in a princess costume again, and the next we could cry because soon enough we'll be shopping for prom dresses.

It may also help to see this moment through a child's eyes. Play-Doh, when you're two, can be truly exciting. We owe it to our kids not to make them grow up too fast. Especially from repeat mothers, this sentiment repeatedly came up in our interviews: It's important to realize that life is not a race. Each month, each year, is made up of many small periods that, in hindsight, race by. "New parents experience that whole competitive thing—he's eight months; oh, is he crawling?" one mother, Yuting, with a fifteen-year-old daughter and an eight-month-old son, told us. "This time around we just don't care. We're gaga over him. Some days I think, oh, maybe he should be on his tummy, but when we come home to him, all we want to do is hold him. He'll walk someday."

DIRTY LITTLE SECRET

I like to go to Starbucks alone. I like the adult sippy cup. I get to drink the whole coffee while it's still hot without interruption. My "latte name" is Kim, and in my mind she's still single and living in the city with *no* kids.

Since our two-year-old daughter was born, we've tried to remember childhood is a journey, not a race. It's posted in her room. Still, my husband encourages her to write, to spell, and I say, "Let's try to appreciate the little things, let's try not to worry about her walking and talking and moving forward."

CARRIE / 2 CHILDREN, HOUSTON, TX

Seeing my child show empathy and a moment of kindness is magical. For example, we had to put one of our dogs to sleep. Our dog was lying in my lap, and I totally lost it, and my three-year-old pulled my face to his face with his hands, and he said, "It's OK, Mommy. It's OK." It just makes you feel so good that you're raising a good human being.

PIPER / 2 CHILDREN, SAN DIEGO, CA

My mom keeps reminding me to just slow down and cherish it because it goes by so fast. Experience this. Many times I wish him to be older so it will be easier, but she reminds me to just treasure this time.

KAYLA / 1 CHILD, PORT ANGELES, WA

7 ways

to enjoy the here and now

1. Living in the moment means readjusting some of your expectations.

2. Don't fight the stage you're in. If it's a challenging phase, know that it will pass quickly. If you're in a blissful phase, cherish it, because it will also pass quickly.

3. Every moment is a valuable moment, no matter how seemingly mundane. Some moms use folding the laundry as their time for meditation. Maybe there's a task you don't love—doing the dishes or driving your kids to school—that you can turn into something meaningful.

4. Look at things through your child's eyes and your world will change. The simple things that inspire them—pebbles or bubbles or birds—can stop us in our tracks and inspire us, too.

5. Just *be*. Right now. We focus on the doing so much of the time that we forget to acknowledge our blessings.

6. Remember, what feels so important now—say, racing home from the park to make sure naps begin on time—will later feel inconsequential.

7. The simple, basic rituals are what will be imprinted on your children forever. Rather than the great big flashy fifth birthday parties, what they'll carry with them are the peanut butter and jelly sandwiches you two shared every day after school.

CHAPTER 10

WHERE DO WE GO FROM HERE?

. . .